B(

HAUNTINGS BY TROY TAYLOR

How does Troy Taylor continue to produce one quality book after another? Perhaps only the spirits know for sure! HAUNTED ILLINOIS is truly another top-notch, in-depth look at the Land of Lincoln. I highly recommend this book to anyone interested in Illinois ghost stories, as it goes to show that ghosts can be found anywhere throughout the state!

DALE KACZMAREK, Author of WINDY CITY GHOSTS

Troy Taylor has done it yet again. In HAUNTED ILLINOIS, the author has hit that rare (and delightful) middle ground between fascinating paranormal research and compelling storytelling. His stories will put you on the edge of your seat and his insights into the supernatural will keep you there. A rare and delightful find and an absolute must-read from one of the best ghost authors writing today.

MARK MERIMAN, Author of HAUNTED INDIANA and SCHOOL SPIRITS

We have read all of the books on Civil War haunts and SPIRITS OF THE CIVIL WAR is the best one ever! It has it all from the history to hauntings and both familiar and little-known ones. This is a must-read for any Civil War buff and for anyone who believes the war continues on in the afterlife! We're not sure how Troy Taylor's going to top this one... but we'll be waiting!

ROB AND ANNE WLORDARSKI, Authors of HAUNTED ALCATRAZ and SOUTHERN FRIED SPIRITS

Troy Taylor has brought a new level of professionalism to the field with the GHOST HUNTER'S GUIDEBOOK, which stands as the best and most authoritative book written to date on ghost investigation. Both beginners and experienced investigators should make this book their bible... it gives the straight savvy...the material is grounded, practical and informative. It comes as no surprise that Taylor's book has gained international praise, including from some of England's most discerning ghost investigators. "Thoroughly recommended," says Alan Murdie, chairman of the distinguished Ghost Club of London. I couldn't agree more.

ROSEMARY ELLEN GUILEY, Author of THE ENCYCLOPEDIA OF GHOSTS & SPIRITS

The text of this manual (THE GHOST HUNTER'S GUIDEBOOK) offers a wealth of modern and really valuable information regarding sophisticated detection equipment and investigation procedures and methods... should become essential reading for anyone in the field of paranormal research, whatever their level of interest or knowledge on the subject.

ANDREW GREEN, Author and British Ghost Researcher

OTHER WORKS BY TROY TAYLOR

HAUNTED ILLINOIS (1999)
SPIRITS OF THE CIVIL WAR (1999)
THE GHOST HUNTER'S GUIDEBOOK (1999)
SEASON OF THE WITCH (1999)
HAUNTED ALTON (2000)

THE HAUNTED DECATUR SERIES
HAUNTED DECATUR (1995)
MORE HAUNTED DECATUR (1996)
GHOSTS OF MILLIKIN (1996)
WHERE THE DEAD WALK (1997)
DARK HARVEST (1997)
HAUNTED DECATUR REVISITED (2000)

GHOSTS OF SPRINGFIELD (1997)
THE GHOST HUNTER'S HANDBOOK (1997)
THE NEW GHOST HUNTER'S HANDBOOK (1998)
GHOSTS OF LITTLE EGYPT (1998)

FILMS, DOCUMENTARIES & TOURS
HAUNTED DECATUR (1996)
SCARY PRAIRIE FIRES (1996)
ADVENTURES BEYOND: AMERICA'S MOST HAUNTED (1997)
GHOST WATERS (1999)
BEYOND HUMAN SENSES (1999)
HAUNTED MUSIC CITY: NASHVILLE GHOSTS (2000)
NIGHT VISITORS (1999)
THE ST. FRANCISVILLE EXPERIMENT (2000)

HAUNTED DECATUR TOURS (1994 - 1998)
HAUNTED DECATUR TOURS (GUEST HOST) (2000)
HISTORY & HAUNTINGS TOURS OF ST. CHARLES (1999)
HISTORY & HAUNTINGS TOURS OF ALTON (1999-2000)

Haunted New Orleans

Ghosts & Hauntings of the Crescent City
By Troy Taylor

- A Whitechapel Productions Press Book -

This book is dedicated to the writers and researchers who taught me through their own examples that history and ghost stories go hand in hand... one cannot exist without the other. Also, to Richard Winer, whose stories of ghosts inspired me during my early years and set my own career into motion.

And, of course, to Amy... without whom no book would be possible. My devotion to her is one of the few things in my life that I never question.

Original Cover Artwork Designed by
Michael Schwab, M & S Graphics & Troy Taylor
Visit M & S Graphics at www.manyhorses.com

This book is Published by
- WHITECHAPEL PRODUCTIONS PRESS -
A DIVISION OF THE HISTORY & HAUNTINGS BOOK CO.
515 EAST THIRD STREET - ALTON, ILLINOIS - 62002
(618) 465-1086 / 1-888-GHOSTLY
Visit us on the Internet at www.prairieghosts.com

First Printing - October 2000
ISBN: 1-892523-11-6

Printed in the United States of America

- Haunted New Orleans -

Take a hundred of the most enthusiastic ghost hunters and ask them to name America's most haunted city. Most will spring to their feet yelling "New Orleans"!
RICHARD WINER in HAUNTED HOUSES

At the end of the long and winding river is America strangest, most exciting and certainly most haunted, city... New Orleans. No city in this country has the dark and checkered background of the Crescent City. It is a background that has bred more than its share of ghosts!
From THE HAUNTING OF AMERICA

The sights and sounds of this most exotic of all southern cities are unlike those of any other place on earth.... the ghosts and haunted places of New Orleans are also unique. The stories have a definite strain of the macabre, yet their undeniable romanticism attests to the duality of this city's personality... the mysterious, chilling legacy of voodoo and slavery and, at the same time, the glamour and excitement typified by Mardi Gras and the revelries of Bourbon Street.
MICHAEL NORMAN & BETH SCOTT in HAUNTED AMERICA

That the charm and beauty of this old city is wrapped in the somber garments of hate, fear and misery is hardly surprising... violence, slavery, pirates, and war were its destiny all the while its beautiful homes were being constructed.
These houses remember. Practically every courtyard in the French Quarter, hiding behind its wrought iron gates, claims a hidden body or a tragic crime. Any winding staircase with its graceful curves may climb to a room in which someone was hidden against his will, in which a crying spirit attempts now to make its presence known.
SUSY SMITH in PROMINENT AMERICAN GHOSTS

In New Orleans alone... there are enough legends to fill volumes.
JEANNE deLAVIGNE in GHOST STORIES OF OLD NEW ORLEANS

†

– Haunted New Orleans Table of Contents –

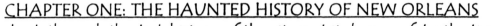

Introduction
Welcome to Haunted
New Orleans

This book has taken me more than 20 years to write.

That's not to say that I have been working on it for the past two decades, but actually that I first dreamed of writing it just about 20 years ago, when I was first introduced to both ghosts and to the strange and magical city of New Orleans. At that time, I had just reached the impressionable age of 13. Childhood seemed to be falling away behind me and ahead of me was the future... a time about which I could only wonder. What did I plan to do with my life? I had no idea.

At that awkward age, I was one of those kids (everyone seems to know at least one) who could always be found with his nose buried in a book. I didn't really care what I was reading, as long as it could transport me somewhere else and preferably, give me a good scare or two along the way.

You see, in addition to being an avid reader, I was also the kid at your school who was obsessed with monsters, ghosts, horror movies and anything else that was sure to creep out my friends or incur the wrath of my teachers. I can't count the number of times that my monster magazines were confiscated by some well-meaning (but very misguided) educator or the number of disapproving glances that I received while poring over an already dog-eared copy of a new horror novel.

It was at this same time that I also discovered sometimes truth can be stranger than fiction. I had always been mildly interested in the realm of ghosts and the supernatural. As far back as my grade school years, I can recall reading books with titles like "True Ghost Stories", but no book made an impression on me like the one that I bought when I was 13.

I was in a local bookstore one day when I ran across a paperback book with a vivid blue house on the cover. The gothic-looking mansion had one window glowing eerily on an upper floor and you had no need to read the title of the book to know the subject of the book was a spooky one. The name of this particular book though was HAUNTED HOUSES. It had been written by a man named Richard Winer and by Nancy Osborn. I remember picking it up and reading the back of the book and despite the catchy descriptive text, there was one section of it that really got my attention. EVERY TOUR OF THE UNEXPLAINABLE IN THIS BOOK, it read, IS BASED ON DOCUMENTED INVESTIGATION.

This was no recounting of legends or ghost stories, I realized, this was the real thing. I flipped open the book and looked over the contents and the photographs it contained. I made a quick decision that I needed to own this book and I quickly paid for it. I spent the rest of the family shopping trip sitting in the car, already devouring my latest find.

In the weeks that followed, I read and re-read the book several times. I couldn't get enough of it. The horror novels that had so previously fascinated me could not compare with the investigations of Mr. Winer and Ms. Osborn. They weren't just reading about ghosts, they were actually going out and finding them. Was such a thing possible... that someone could actually do this for a living?

I can't remember how many times I must have read that book during the summer months that followed. My favorite sections had become worn and battered, but the rest of the book was becoming a little tattered as well. I loved the tales of the Bell Witch, the Winchester House, Alcatraz and others, but there was one section of the book that kept my interest more than any other and that was the chapter on New Orleans. It never failed to both chill and amaze me. I vowed that someday I would visit the city and I would find every single spot that was told about in the book. Someday.....

But that day came sooner that I could have ever imagined. A short time later, my parents announced the destination for our summer vacation. It was, you guessed it, New Orleans! Within a few weeks, I was actually walking the streets of the French Quarter and experiencing the place that Richard Winer had called "America's most haunted city". Thankfully, my parents took me to visit the places listed in HAUNTED HOUSES, which was clutched tightly in my hand during our entire visit, and I became entranced with New Orleans. On a side note, I have never returned to New Orleans without that worn-out book packed away in my luggage.

That book, and that visit to New Orleans, changed my entire life. After that, I became determined to not only become a writer, but a writer about ghosts. In my way of thinking, Richard Winer made his living traveling all over the country, writing about haunted houses. I would, I announced, do the same thing. In 1995, that vow became true and I published my first book. It was not about New Orleans, but about the town where I lived. I had not yet traveled all over America in search of ghosts... but I was beginning my journey.

Now, with 14 other books having already been written, I still feel my journey is far from complete. I have many other haunted destinations that I have yet to write about, but one of the most important to me is New Orleans. Since that first trip, I have since visited the city a number of times but it has never lost that initial magic for me. I still find New Orleans to be that dark and enthralling city that it was two decades ago. Every time that I would visit, I would tell myself that a book needs to be written about my travels here... and about the ghosts that linger in this place. Finally, after a recent visit, I went away with a nagging feeling inside of me. I had waited all of these years and now it was time for me to put my pen to paper and begin my HAUNTED NEW ORLEANS.

Now, having said all of that, I want to back up and say that in no way do I consider myself "destined" to write the greatest book ever written about New Orleans. There have been many wonderful books written about the city and this is far from the first (and will most likely not be the last) to be written about her ghosts and hauntings. This book was not written to be better than any of the others, merely different. With that said, I should also confess that if no single other person reads this book, I will still feel that I have accomplished something by writing it. My own journey to New Orleans will have been completed and I can say that I have finally been able to do something that I have always wanted to do. Perhaps more than for anyone else, the book you are (hopefully) holding in your hands was written for me.

However, I don't feel that the pages that follow will disappoint you. I have managed to collect stories of hauntings and dark history that are both familiar and unfamiliar, have been lost or forgotten by time and most of all, are uniquely a part of the haunted history of New Orleans. There are all sorts of tales of hauntings and strange events, including stories of haunted houses, terrifying locations, bizarre legends, bloody history and some which are not ghost stories at all... but are so unusual that they had to be included anyway.

Can I say that each one of these fantastic stories is true? I cannot tell you that, although each one of them was told to me, another author, or someone else as the truth. The stories presented in this book are presented here as "real" stories, told by "real" people, however, I will leave the truth of each tale for you to decide upon for yourself.

In nearly every book I write, I always like to take the reader along on another short trip before beginning the journey in the heart of the book itself. That small trip always involves the "lore" of the ghosts themselves. What sort of hauntings can the reader expect to find in the dark places ahead?

There are many theories and ideas out there as to what, or who, ghosts actually are and why they choose to haunt the places they do. I can't tell you that I know everything about ghosts because I don't believe there are any "experts" when it comes to the supernatural. I usually prefer the term "knowledgeable", because no one can say what ghosts really are, they can only describe their own experiences with these elusive creatures.

People often ask me if I have seen a ghost? I would still have to say that I'm not for sure. I have certainly seen and experienced a lot of things that I cannot explain, but seeing a ghost isn't the only way to experience them. I have had some strange encounters over the years, all over the country, which I don't have easy explanations for!

But what are ghosts? And what is a haunting? And how do these things relate to the ghostly locations in this book?

First of all, what exactly is a haunting?

It is defined as being the repeated manifestation of strange and inexplicable sensory phenomena at a certain location. There are no general patterns to hauntings, which is what makes them so hard to define. Some phenomena may manifest on occasion or even continually for periods which last from several days to centuries; others may only occur on certain anniversaries; and others may make no sense whatsoever.

The general public assumes that hauntings involve apparitions, or ghosts, of the dead, but in fact, apparitions are connected to only a minority of cases. Most hauntings involve noises like phantom footsteps; strange, unexplainable sounds; tapping; knocking sounds; strange smells; and sensations like the cold prickling of the skin, chilling breezes and even the feeling of being touched by an invisible hand. Other hauntings involve poltergeist-like activity such as furniture and solid objects being moved about; broken glass; doors which open and close by themselves; and the paranormal manipulation of lights and electrical devices.

While attempts have been made to try and categorize certain types of hauntings (as you'll soon see) many locations seem to defy this labeling and manifest a variety and a combination of different types. In fact, it has been my experience that some locations seem to act as catalyst for activity, causing visitors to manifest their own unconscious phenomena... giving rise to accounts which don't fit into any categories at all.

The two different types of hauntings that seem to be most commonly reported are what we call the "intelligent haunting" and the "residual haunting".

The intelligent spirit is everyone's traditional idea of a ghost. It is a lost personality, or spirit, that for some reason did not pass over to the other side at the moment of death. It shows an intelligence and a consciousness and often interacts with people. It is the most widely accepted kind of paranormal activity because it is the easiest to understand. It is there because of a connection to the site or to the people at the location.

This ghost is the personality of a once living person who stayed behind in our world. This sometimes happens in the case of a murder, a traumatic event, or because of some unfinished business which was left undone in a person's life. At the time of death, this spirit refused to cross over to the other side because of these events. There is also a good chance that this spirit does not even realize that it has died, which could happen if the death was sudden or unexpected.

If this sounds too much for you to believe, look at this way. This spirit is simply the personality, or soul, of someone who once lived. If you can accept the idea that each person is made up of a personality, making us who we are, then it is not too much of a stretch to consider the idea that this personality lives on. There is no scientific proof that says that the personality even exists... yet most people believe that it does. So who is to say that this personality, which again, science cannot say even exists, will not exist outside of the body at the time of our physical death?

If you are a religious person, you probably believe that your soul goes on to heaven, or some better place, when you die.... but what if some of them don't? What if some of these spirits still walk the earth?

It makes you wonder, doesn't it?

Another type of haunting that is often reported has nothing to do with intelligent, or conscious, spirits at all. It is more common than people think and you might be surprised as to how many ghost stories that you have heard over the years just may fit into this category. This haunting is both unexplainable and fascinating..... and can be downright spooky too!

This type of haunting is called a "residual haunting" and the easiest way to explain it is to compare it to an old film loop, meaning that it is a scene which is replayed over and over again through the years. These hauntings are really just a piece of time that is stuck in place. Many haunted places experience events that may imprint themselves on the atmosphere of a place in a way that we don't yet understand. This event suddenly discharges and plays itself at various times... thus resulting in a place being labeled as haunted.

These "phantom" events are not necessarily just visual either. They are often replayed as sounds and noises that cannot be explained, like footsteps that go up and down the stairs when no one is there. They can also sometimes appear as smells or other sensory events.

Often the sounds and images "recorded" are related to traumatic events that took place at the location and caused what might be called a "psychic disturbance". In other situations, they have been events or actions repeated over and over again to cause the impression. Researchers have suggested that there exist so many haunted staircases because of the number of times that people go up and down them and the amount of energy expended in doing so.

These locations act as giant storage batteries, saving up the impressions of sights and sounds from the past. Then, as the years go by, these impressions appear again as though a film projector has started to run. These types of ghosts do not interact with people and usually are observed (or heard) doing the same things over and over again. Eventually, many of these hauntings wear down and fade away, while others continue for eternity.

No one is really sure how these types of hauntings take place but there is little doubt that they exist.... as you'll see later in the book. In the following pages and chapters, this type of haunting will be seen over and over again. Admittedly, this is not the usual idea of a ghost but no one can deny that these hauntings belong in the realm of the unexplained. Ghosts? Perhaps not.... but ghostly, nonetheless!

So how do we know that ghosts are real?

Remember that just because you have never seen a ghost does not mean that they don't exist. Belief has little or nothing to do with being able to see them. When ghosts are seen, it is usually because they are "all in the head" of the person who sees them.

That doesn't mean that ghosts are a hallucination though. We must remember that one part of our perception uses our five senses and the other part is the processing of those senses, which is done by our brain. The brain only allows us to see what it thinks we can handle and will add and subtract information depending on what it is processing.

Science tells us that the human eye does not see things the way they really are.... it takes the brain to process the information gathered by the eye and then present it to our conscious minds in a way that we can understand.

It's possible that our conscious minds do not allow us to see ghosts. Why? I have often thought that perhaps our culture and our societal beliefs simply rebel against the very idea of ghosts, rendering them consciously invisible to us. This might be why so many ghost sightings are "accidental", as the ghost slips through our mental screening process. This results in an ordinary person seeing a ghost.

Here's another way to explain it..... Just imagine for a moment that all around you are millions of radio waves, passing by you without a sound. If you turn on a radio, and tune it to the right station, you will suddenly be able to hear one of the radio waves that moments before was silent. Seeing a ghost for the ordinary person is much the same thing. Just for a moment, you might be somehow "tuned to the right station" and see something that may have existed already, although was inexplicably unseen.

So, what do you think? Do you find this all hard to believe?
Or are you open to the possibility that ghosts might be real?
Is New Orleans really a haunted and mysterious place?

If you are a skeptical reader, you are probably already thinking that ghosts are most certainly the figments of our imagination. Such stories and tales are merely the creations of fools, drunkards and folklorists. You might even finish this book, but most likely even then, you will still be unable to accept the fact that ghosts may exist. If you are this person, I can only hope to entertain you with the history, and what you will consider the folklore, of the city of New Orleans.

But don't be so sure that you have all of the answers...

Can you say for sure that ghosts aren't real? Are you totally convinced that spirits do not wander the streets of New Orleans? Those are the questions that you really have to ask yourself.... and try doing it some night while you are walking alone down some shadowy street in the Vieux Carre.

Is that whispering sound you hear really the wind blowing down the street....or the voice of Pere Dagobert still crying for the souls of the dead?

Is that merely a patch of fog that you see darting into a secluded courtyard.... or could it be one of the tortured slaves of Madame LaLaurie, seeking his revenge?

Is that naked figure on the rooftop merely some late night reveler... or could it be the ghost of a beautiful octoroon mistress who freezes in the night for her lover?

Is that rustling that you hear really just the passing breeze... or are those footsteps coming up behind you?

If you turn to look, then you may not be totally convinced that ghosts are a part of our fanciful fiction. You may have to consider that we don't have all of the answers, that the unknown is still out there, beckoning to us......

Sit back, relax, put an old jazz record on the turntable and get ready to take a journey... one that will lead you back over the centuries and to another time and place. Take my hand as I light the lamp and together, we'll discover a place where the next world exists just below the surface of this one.

Welcome to Haunted New Orleans.

Troy Taylor
June 2000

- Haunted New Orleans -

The name of "New Orleans" conjures up a succulent variety of images, from the soft sounds of jazz to whirring ceiling fans, wrought iron gates, and hot, spicy food. Along the swollen Mississippi River, the city dozes, only to come alive at night with the revelry of its people and the blare of music and laughter from Bourbon Street and the French Quarter.

These are the images of New Orleans that many people think of... but there is another side to the city as well, an underbelly and a darkness that is as carefully hidden as the gates to the small courtyards that lurk between buildings in the Quarter. This dark side is there, just like the spectacular gardens and courtyards, but you have to know where to look for it. Even if you don't see it though, it's liable to sneak out and surprise you when you least expect it.

The dark side of New Orleans is as compelling as the chicory-laced coffee and the delicious "beignets" however.... it's a dark side which is filled with the seductive images of voodoo, vampires and ghosts. Only in New Orleans could darkness and death seem so appealing!

✝

Chapter One
The Haunted History of New Orleans

It is impossible for mere words to paint a complete picture of the city that is New Orleans. This book might best be used as a travel guide to ghosts and haunted history, and one that is carried in hand while wandering the streets of the French Quarter and beyond.

For those who journey no further than the comfort of their armchair though, a chronicle of the city must be created.... for to understand the ghosts of New Orleans, we must take a dark journey back into the city's troubled and blood-drenched past.

The first colonists to arrive in New Orleans were of French origin. They came to this hot and swampy place in the early 1700's, preceded only by the explorers. The explorers included men like LaSalle, who came down the Mississippi River in 1682 and claimed the land where the river ended for France. In 1699, two French-Canadian explorers named Pierre le Moyne and Jean Baptiste le Moyne sailed in from the Caribbean and landed on a tiny bayou they called Pointe du Mardi Gras as the Catholic holiday of Fat Tuesday was to fall the next day.

It was not all swashbuckling adventure though. Exploring the New World was an expensive proposition and by 1700 the French were broke. The Bourbons of France were approached by a Scottish man named John Law, who created a New World company in which the French could invest and thereby settle the Lower Mississippi Valley. In reality, the plan was a scheme to bilk money from the investors in return for selling them Louisiana. Law was given a monopoly on trade as well. Later, when it turned out that Law's company was merely and early version of a "pyramid scheme", many of the settlers decided to stay on anyway.

During the first year of Law's operation, he decided that a town should be founded at a spot that could be reached from both Lake Pontchartrain and the Mississippi. In 1718, this town became La Nouvelle Orleans.

Development of the city began that year, but work was slow, thanks to brutal heat and the rising and falling waters of the Mississippi. There was talk of moving the city because of the danger of flooding, so levees were constructed, which spread out as the city and the plantations of the area grew. The mouth of the Mississippi was considered a dangerous place for other reasons as well. In many early documents, writers spoke of the monsters that dwelt in the murky waters and the Indian legends told of gigantic beasts that waited to spring upon unwary travelers. "May God preserve us from the crocodiles!", wrote Father Louis Hennepin.

At the same time, John Law was attempting to fulfill his promises to investors that he would have the colony settled with 6,000 settlers and 3,000 slaves by 1727. The biggest problem seemed to be the shortage of women. "The white men," wrote the colony's Governor Bienville," are running in the woods after the Indian girls". Around 1720, one solution to cure the shortage of women was arrived at when the jails of Paris were emptied of prostitutes. The "ladies of the evening" were given a choice... serve their term in prison or become a colonist in Louisiana. Those who chose the New World quickly became the wives of the men most starved for female companionship.

The prisons were emptied of others as well. Many thieves, vagabonds, deserters and smugglers also chose to come to Louisiana to avoid prison time, along with aristocrats, indicted for some wrongdoing or another, who chose New Orleans over the Bastille.

In addition to a lack of women, there was also a lack of education and medical care in New Orleans. Finally, Governor Bienville coaxed the Sisters of Ursuline to come from France and assist the new city. The first Ursulines arrived in 1727 and set to work caring for orphans, operating a school, setting up a free hospital and instructing slaves for baptism. They also provided a safe haven for the "casket girls", young middle class girls who had come in answer to the call for suitable wives. The young women were so-named (depending on the story you hear) for either the distinctive shaped hats they wore, or for the government-issued casket-shaped chests of clothes and linen they brought with them. The first of the "casket girls" arrived in 1728 and they continued to come until 1751, marrying those single male colonists who had been unable to snag one of the "professional" girls who had been sent from the Paris jails a few years before.

But things were far from perfect in New Orleans. There was great unrest among the local Chickasaw Indian tribes, although Governor Bienville had managed to gain the respect of the Indians for France. Thanks to political problems though, Bienville was eventually recalled to France and the grudging peace with the Indians slowly began to deteriorate. In 1729, Natchez Indians, allies of the Chickasaw, attacked Fort Rosalie at Natchez, slaughtering about 250 and kidnapping 450 women, children and slaves.

The nearby Indian attacks, combined with the political disorder of the time, caused the investors in John Law's company to petition France to get rid of the unprofitable Louisiana colony. And so they did, leaving behind a sturdy and hard-bitten group of 7,000 colonists with a thriving business industry but an uncertain future.

In 1762, France passed the ownership of Louisiana to Spain in the secret Treaty of Fontainebleau. That same year, Spain entered the Seven Years War (the European arm of the

The Vieux Carre

The original neighborhood of New Orleans still stands today in the same location that it did centuries ago when settlers hacked away palmetto thickets to make room for their ramshackle house. It remains the beating heart of Old New Orleans.

The Vieux Carre (French Quarter) came into existence in 1721 when the New Orleans governor commissioned a French engineer named Adrien du Pauger to create a grid of European-style streets and a grand public square for the colony. To do this, he had to convince the settlers to tear down their homes and rebuild them into the new design. Although he faced a challenge, a 66-square-block network of streets was soon established.

The wooden buildings that filled the area were destroyed by fire on March 21, 1788. When the city was rebuilt, the Spanish governor ordered many improvements, including street lights and a drainage canal along Carondelet Street. It was at this point that the city became the French Quarter that we know today.

Then, in 1793 and 1794, the new city was struck by three hurricanes and in 1794, another terrible fire swept through the city and destroyed most of the remaining French homes. It wiped out almost 200 of the wooden buildings, mostly private homes, in less than 3 hours.

In spite of this, the Vieux Carre was again rebuilt and it remains today as a symbol of the heartiness of the people of Old New Orleans.

French and Indian War) just in time to share defeat with France. As part of the Treaty of Paris at the end of the war, France had to give up its holdings in North America... however they had just given New Orleans and Louisiana to Spain the year before. No one in Louisiana had any indication of this for months, when suddenly, the colonists found themselves under the control of the much-hated Governor Don Antonio de Ulloa.

In 1768, 600 New Orleans citizens mounted the first revolutionary expedition of Americans against a European government. The ranks were made up of Acadians (French-speaking immigrants from Canada), who had been told they were going to be sold into slavery by the Spanish and German immigrants. They also believed the Spanish were going to default on money owed to John Law's company. By November 1, Don Antonio had escaped to Cuba and the rebels took prisoner his three aides.

His Majesty Carlos of Spain did not find this event amusing in the least and sent a 2,600 man mercenary force to New Orleans to re-take the city. Don Alexander O'Reilly, an Irishman in the service of Spain, led the army. He later earned the nickname "Bloody O'Reilly" after he sent all of the revolutionaries before the firing squad.

The Spanish remained in control of the city for a number of years after these events but many changes were coming to the region.

The refugees and adventurers of many nations were beginning to arrive in New Orleans. Restlessness was especially being felt on the American continent as those with a hunger for a new life began pressing westward from the colonies.

In 1765, the first shiploads of Acadians had arrived in New Orleans after being exiled and driven out of their homes in Nova Scotia. These simple farming people, of French origin, were fiercely protective of their freedom and had led the uprising against Spain in 1768. They remained in New Orleans for awhile but soon moved on into the bayous north and west of the city. They brought their language and customs into the swamps and back country and eventually, their name was slurred into the word "Cajun". The descendants of these original settlers continue to thrive in this region today.

Another great, and catastrophic, change came in March 1788 when the city of New Orleans was destroyed by fire. As the city was constructed almost entirely of wood, the flames quickly devoured it. The fire started on Good Friday and because of the holiday, the Capuchin monks refused to allow the church bells to ring a warning to the populace. As a result, the fire was out of control before enough men could be gathered to try and stop it. Section after section of the city was destroyed, including the government house, the jails, the residences, the business section, the church and ironically, even the monastery of the monks who had refused the bells to be sounded. Only a row of houses along the levee was spared, along with the Ursuline Convent that had been built from brick and tile. The convent records say that the building was saved "by a miracle."

The city that fell in the fire was a congested French community of poorly built wooden homes that had been badly arranged. Thanks to the Spanish, the city that took its place is still the Vieux Carre that we know today. As the rebuilding began, the Spanish architects and builders took part in the construction. The city that came from the ashes was one of brick and plaster, with heavy arches and roofs of tile. The buildings were erected flush against the sidewalks, balconies overhung the streets and shaded courtyards were placed between and behind the stately homes, hiding banana trees, fountains and flowers. New homes and businesses began to appear and some would say that the fire was actually a blessing to the city.

A prominent member of the community was a man named Don Andres Almonaster y Roxas. He was a Spaniard of noble birth and the richest man in New Orleans. He was vexed by the fire and declared that he would build a new church for the city, a new hospital, a new government building and a monastery for the Capuchins. He donated the money and the materials and these three buildings still stand at the edge of Jackson Square today. In 1850, renovations were made to the roofs of the buildings that flank the cathedral and the central spire was added to the church of St. Louis, but basically, they are the same buildings that Don Almonaster completed in 1795. He is now buried near the altar in the Cathedral.

Not long after the city had recovered from fire, it faced another threat... one created by man and one that was perhaps even darker than anything nature could imagine.

Charles III had died in Spain and Charles IV, a weak and incompetent king, had succeeded him. Soon after his taking of the throne, Father Antonio de Sedella was sent by his superiors to Louisiana as a representative of the Holy Roman Inquisition. Having heard of the brutality being carried out by the Inquisition in Europe, the Louisiana Governor was determined that no such acts would take place in New Orleans. When Father Antonio arrived in New Orleans, he was captured by soldiers in the night and swiftly put aboard another vessel bound for Spain. The entire incident was kept secret and somehow, New Orleans managed to avoid the horror of the Spanish Inquisition..... or did it?

According to author Lyle Saxon, some strange things were discovered when an old jail near the Cathedral was torn down many years after the incident. Newspaper accounts cited that secret rooms, iron instruments of torture and signs that a private court had held meetings were found in the jail. The discovery was never explained. In addition, old newspaper accounts also told of a secret passage that led from the rear of the Cathedral and ended near the jail. The story soon vanished from the newspapers and was never spoken of again. At any rate, Saxon wrote, there is no "official" record of the Inquisition in Louisiana.

The first real hope for the French settlers in New Orleans that they might someday be again governed by France came in the 1790's, when the events taking place during the French Revolution began to reach the colony. Many of the residents became filled with patriotism and there were cries for "liberty" in the theaters and public places. When the news of the execution of Louis XVI reached New Orleans, there was open celebration. The Spanish Governor, fearing another uprising, had six prominent French leaders arrested and they were exiled to Cuba for one year. He also began to fortify the city, erecting a masonry wall around the original Vieux Carre with stockades at the corners. Two of them faced the river and two faced the swamps beyond the city. The fortifications, he explained, were not to protect New Orleans from the French, but from the Americans, from whom he feared an invasion was eminent.

The Governor, Cardondelet, was succeeded in 1797 by Don Manuel Gayoso de Lemos, beginning the "golden age" of the Spanish in New Orleans. While this period only lasted for two years, it marks a time when the city truly began to grow and prosper and after this, it would forever be known as the most important port on the Caribbean.

In 1800, the people of New Orleans discovered that the city had been given back to Napoleon of France as a result of the secret Treaty of San Ildefonso. But Napoleon was busy that year conquering the Turks, the Austrians and the Italians, plus ending a slave uprising on St. Domingue. Since New Orleans was struck with a terrible yellow fever epidemic, he allowed the Spanish to continue governing the colony.

Soon, another group began to influence the culture of the city. The residents called them the "Kaintocks" and these buckskin-clad American frontiersmen descended on the city in force. The shrewd Americans had realized the potential of the thriving port of the city and began bringing keelboats loaded with goods down the Mississippi.

By 1804, the city would belong to America. Napoleon needed money and thanks to some stiff bargaining by President Thomas Jefferson, the Louisiana Territory, which was over 600 million acres, was soon in the possession of the United States. The cost of the territory, which stretched from the Mississippi to the Pacific Ocean, was around $15 million, which makes it one of the greatest land deals in history!

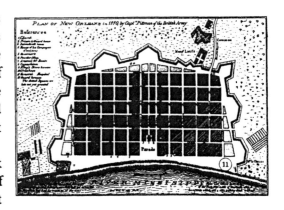

The transfer of New Orleans took place on the balcony of the Cabildo off Jackson Square. The city, along with the rest of the Louisiana Territory, was formally given to General Wilkinson and W.C.C. Claiborne, the commissioners appointed by President Jefferson.

New Orleans was now officially an American city... a fact that was met with dismay by the people of New Orleans. The city considered itself highly civilized and equated the word "American" with "Barbarian". The only Americans the Creole residents of the city were familiar with were the rough

VIEW OF NEW ORLEANS IN 1719.

The quartiers des Bourgeois (people quarters) consisted of several clusters of small wooden buildings enclosed by levees, and, for three months of the year usually, from the 25th of March until 4th of June there quartiers were transformed into island by the overflow from the river. The drainage was effected though a canal dug in the rear.

frontiersmen and the even more intolerable flatboatmen. These men gave endless trouble to the police for fighting and public drunkenness and in addition, spoke an uncouth and alien language. This was the general impression of all Americans and the arrival of the first settlers from the United States did little to change this way of thinking. Little business was conducted between the two groups and the American women were snubbed by the Creole ladies.

Because of this, the Americans created a society of their own and eventually created their own city as well, outside of the boundaries of the Vieux Carre. Altercations between the Creole and the Americans were not infrequent and at last, a boundary was created between the two societies. A strip of land between the French Quarter and the American section was designated as a "neutral ground" by an act of Congress in 1807. It later became known as Canal Street.

By 1810, with its mixture of French and Spanish speaking Creoles, Anglo- Americans, slaves and free people of color, New Orleans was established as the largest city in the South and the fifth largest city in America. The city had truly come into its own, a fact that was proven in 1812 when the steamboat NEW ORLEANS arrived in port and ushered in a new age for the city, and a new period of prosperity. The aristocrats of the city filled their lavish mansions with the finest Persian rugs, crystal chandeliers, and the best French wines that money could buy.

However, luxuries aside, New Orleans was not a place for the weak. Located below sea level, in a hot and humid climate, it was a place of oppressive humidity from June to October and was infested with mosquitoes. The city was often hit with terrible cholera and tropical illness epidemics and was labeled a "damp grave" for those foolish enough to live here.

And that's not to mention the hurricanes, thunderstorms from the Gulf of Mexico, and the frequent floods. The spring flooding would usually pour about two feet of muddy water and debris into the city, not to mention snakes and rats. New levees were constructed each time the devastation would hit the city but each time, the damage was horrible.

In 1832, New Orleans was savaged by a cholera epidemic and in addition, between 1817 and 1860, there were 23 outbreaks of Yellow Fever. This wicked disease was spread by mosquitoes, which bred in household cisterns. The most serious epidemic of yellow fever hit the city in 1853, sending thousands to higher ground in surrounding cities like Natchez and Mobile. Over 8,000 people died before the cool months of fall arrived. For those not felled by the disease, there was no clue as to what was causing the outbreak. Days of prayer were organized and cannons were blasted each day to break up the clouds over the city, thinking that perhaps they were responsible for the disease.

Hurricanes, floods and Yellow Fever aside, Louisiana would become the 18th state in the Union on April 30, 1812, and barely a month later, Congress declared war on Britain. A few weeks after Mardi Gras in 1814, rumors filled the city that the British were going to attack New Orleans.

The Battle of New Orleans

If there was one thing that could bring together the opposing forces in New Orleans, being the Catholic Creoles and the Protestant Americans, it was a threat from the British. The people of New Orleans, who still considered themselves mostly Spanish or French, were long used to being governed by enemies of Britain. As for the Americans, the bitterness from hard-won independence they had achieved from England still lingered in their not-so-distant memory. The last thing they wanted was to fall under the thumb of the British once again. With this in mind, the Creoles and the Americans began to rally together. The coming battle would be just the catalyst to showcase the bravery of all of the people of New Orleans... if they survived. At this point, the city was defenseless. Word reached New Orleans that the Capitol and the White House in Washington had been burned and that President James Madison was unable to raise an army because the United States Treasury was empty.

The city was nearly in chaos when hope arrived from the north in the form of General Andrew Jackson. The crusty Indian fighter had come to New Orleans already in 1812 when the British first threatened the city. After arriving at the mouth of the Mississippi with his men from Tennessee, he was ordered to disband his army and return home. Disgusted, Jackson fought the Creek Indians before being sent back to New Orleans in 1814.

He arrived in New Orleans in December, only to be confined to his bed with dysentery and a high fever. In spite of his health, he still managed to quickly organize a defense of the city. He imposed martial law and enlisted the aid of every breathing human being who could fire a gun. He soon accepted the assistance of regiments of free people of color, Kentuckians who came downriver on flatboats, Choctaw Indians and of course, pirate brigades under the command of Jean Lafitte and his brother, Pierre.

Of all of the pirates who sailed the Caribbean, preying on merchant and slave ships, there are none who have gained as much fame in New Orleans as Jean Lafitte has. In truth, Lafitte was a minor pirate when compared to others of the day. Operating from the bayous south of New Orleans, he was only saved from the noose because of his aid to General Jackson during the Battle of New Orleans.

The details of his early life are vague, although he was thought to have been born in France in 1780, or on Haiti, depending on the story you hear. By 1809, he and his brother, Pierre, had immigrated to New Orleans, where they operated a blacksmith shop in the Vieux Carre. The business was actually a front for their smuggling operation, which dealt in slaves and stolen goods.

In 1810, Lafitte formed a loose band of pirates, privateers and smugglers who were based in Barataria Bay, located south of the city. Over the next few years, they raided ships in the Gulf of Mexico, concentrating mainly on Spanish galleons and slave traders. Even after slave trading was outlawed in Louisiana, plantation owners attended secret auctions in the bayous and here, merchants were also able to purchase low-cost, plundered goods from the pirates.

Eventually, the secret meetings became too well known and the brothers Lafitte were charged with piracy and illegal trading. Released on bail, they escaped the city and continued their operations. A bounty of $500 was placed on Lafitte's head in 1813 and Jean responded by posting bills advertising a price of $5000 on the governor's head instead!

The disagreement over maritime conditions that led to the War of 1812 erupted and went badly for the Americans. Not only were the invasions of Canada repulsed, but also the fledging American naval captains found themselves blockaded into their own ports by the superior British fleet. At New Orleans, the British wanted to continue the success they had found in Maryland and Washington by attacking New Orleans and disrupting transport on the Mississippi River. In September 1814, British officers offered Jean Lafitte a pardon and a rich reward if he and his pirates would help them attack New Orleans. Lafitte quickly informed the Americans of the impending attack, although it was more likely because of the threat to his New Orleans market than out of any sense of patriotism.

Lafitte's information did not garner him a reward from the Americans though. Instead, Barataria Bay was invaded by American ships, which captured the pirate fleet as it lay at anchor. Lafitte and his men managed to hide out in the swamps until the Navy left and then they reclaimed their settlement.

When Andrew Jackson arrived in New Orleans a short time later, things changed for the pirates. Jackson, having never been accused of being conventional, realized that Lafitte and his men could offer much for the defense of the city. Jackson quickly made a practical offer to Lafitte... help save the city, and his profitable market, and Jackson would see to it that Lafitte was offered a pardon for his crimes. Lafitte agreed and his men manned guns that had been taken from two warships during the fighting.

After the battle, Lafitte was given a full pardon by President Madison a month later. Rather than remain in New Orleans, the new national hero sailed for a new location to continue his piracy. He and his men chose Texas, a lawless frontier region between America and Spanish Mexico. They established a port at Galveston and within a year, the area became a haven for criminals and smugglers. While Lafitte mostly preyed on Spanish ships from Mexico, he made the mistake of attacking several American ships in 1819. This led to an outcry and a naval expedition was dispatched against him.

In 1820, a naval force headed by the USS ENTERPRISE bombarded and destroyed Galveston. Lafitte escaped capture but what became of him is unknown. Most believe that he died in Mexico. In 1976, a historical group erected a monument to the pirate in the village of Dzilam de Bravo on the Yucatan Peninsula. They believe he died of Yellow Fever here in 1826.

Other theories abound. One legend states that Lafitte married and moved to Alton, Illinois, where he buried some of his treasure. This legend mixes with fact in that Pierre Lafitte did move to St. Louis (across the river from Alton) and died there in 1844. According to his children, their uncle had changed his name to John Lafflin and had dropped out of sight.

Perhaps the most unusual legend has Lafitte buried in the Berthoud Cemetery on

Bayou Barataria, but he does not rest here alone. It is said that Lafitte lies side by side with John Paul Jones and Napoleon Bonaparte as well! Lafitte is supposed to have rescued Napoleon from St. Helena and left a double in his place, but the Emperor died on the way to Louisiana. He was buried near Lafitte's hideout at Barataria. Also according to the legend, John Paul Jones joined Lafitte's pirate band and was killed in action. When Lafitte died, his pirates buried him next to the other two fallen heroes. On certain occasions, the stories say, this motley trio of ghosts appears.

And, not surprisingly, this is far from the only location where Lafitte's restless ghost is said to appear. Usually, the stories revolve around some lost bit of treasure that Lafitte is supposed to have buried in the bayous in the region. The tales of buried treasure make pirate ghosts very common as, tradition states, the pirates would often murder a member of their crew when hiding treasure. In that way, his ghost would always guard over the hidden loot. The legends continue to have Jean Lafitte appearing so often around lost treasure that, as Lyle Saxon and Robert Tallant wrote, "it is unlikely he finds time for anything else in the world beyond this one". In one old house, Lafitte supposedly came nightly, pointing a spectral finger at the tiled flooring. When news of the haunting spread, treasure hunters dug up the entire lower floor of the house!

In spite of their legendary standing, Lafitte and his pirates were not the "saviors" of New Orleans as such a position must go to General Andrew Jackson himself. On December 23, 1814 Jackson attacked the British troops who were camped along the banks of the Mississippi. The British forces were led by General Pakenham and although fresh from defeating Napoleon, they suffered a severe blow at the hands of ragtag troops made up of Kentuckian Long Rifles, ill-prepared militia men, Indians, Creoles, free men of color and pirates. The fighting raged back and forth for several bitterly cold days between Christmas and New Years. The British continued to be reinforced with each passing day until they greatly outnumbered the American forces in New Orleans.

On New Year's Day, the British attacked the city's defenses, only to be driven back. Then, on January 8, the final battle took place on the muddy and mist-covered grounds of Chalmette Plantation. The Americans huddled behind bales of straw and cotton and soon began to hear the ghostly sounds of bagpipes and drums coming from the fog. Soon, they were able to see the colors of the Duchess of York's Light Dragoons and the tartans of the 93rd Highlanders. The British troops charged, advancing in tight, efficient lines.

But the combat-hardened troops were no match for the desperate men of New Orleans. The militiamen, the hastily organized regiments and the pirates savagely blasted the British lines without mercy. By later that day, Jackson's army had prevailed, with only 15 men dead and 40 wounded.

The British were not so lucky. The carnage on their side consisted of 858 dead and about 2,500 wounded. They had nowhere to turn for medical care and legend has it that they sought refuge with the Ursuline Sisters, who would turn no one away. The stories say that many enemy troops were hidden within their walls.

Shortly after the battle, news reached the city that the British had signed a peace treaty at Ghent on Christmas Eve, two weeks before the Battle of New Orleans.

The Civil War in New Orleans

By the Civil War era, New Orleans had the largest cotton market in the world and was, by far, the wealthiest city in America. It had been an American city for just over 50 years when it found itself embroiled in war. On February 4, 1861 Senator Judah P. Benjamin announced to Congress that Louisiana had seceded from the Union. The state would stand alone for three entire months until it joined the Confederate States of America.

The decision to secede was not popular with everyone in New Orleans, especially with the merchants who depended on the northern markets to earn their livings. There were also problems raised for the free people of color in the city, who were now at war with a Union that proposed not only the abolition of slavery, but the power to vote and the right of public education for all people of color. However, despite this volatile mixture of emotions, when the war began, it would be General Pierre Gustave Toutant Beauregard and his regiment of Louisiana men who would open fire on Fort Sumter on April 12, 1861.

The war in New Orleans came early and the city spent the greatest amount of the war under Union control, despite being located so far into the enemy territory of the Confederacy. The Union almost immediately began its blockade of the Mississippi River and cut off the city from its imported supplies of flour, paper and coffee. Plans were soon made for the capture of the city itself. The fall of New Orleans would be catastrophic for the Confederacy and would enable the Federal forces to divide the south by controlling the Mississippi.

In April of 1862, a fleet of 24 ships, under command of David G. Farragut, was ordered to sail up river and seize New Orleans. The Confederate defenders did everything they could to stop him. To reach the city, Farragut's ships had to get past Fort Jackson and Fort St. Phillip.

Commander David Dixon Porter, Farragut's younger foster brother, came up with a reckless plan. They would send a collection of small sailing vessels, each bearing a huge mortar, into the harbor and anchor them below the forts so that they could pound the defenses in advance of the fleet. They tried this but after six days of battering, the forts remained standing. Farragut decided on an even more daring scheme..... under the cover of night, they would run past the forts, smash the barricades and steam into New Orleans.

At two o'clock in the morning, Farragut's warships started past the forts. The forts opened fire and the lead ship was hit 42 times. It caught fire but they managed to quench the flames and start forward again. It was a test of sheer will, but the four flagships somehow made it past the forts.

As they approached New Orleans, a makeshift Confederate squadron of 8 ships sailed out to meet them. Farragut sank all but 2 of them and sailed toward New Orleans. Immediately, the city was thrown into a panic. The hungry citizens watched in despair as warehouses of food, cotton and lumber were burned to keep them out of the hands of the enemy. Mobs of looters ran through the streets, stealing anything that could be bartered for food with the conquering northern armies. As the Union fleet approached, New Orleans surrendered without a shot being fired.

After the surrender, Lincoln named Benjamin F. "Spoons" Butler of Massachusetts, the military governor of occupied New Orleans. This occupation would last for 15 years, until April 1877, giving New Orleans the rather dubious honor of suffering through a Reconstruction government longer than any other southern city.

Butler saw no need to be gentle in his position of power in New Orleans and his methods earned him both admiration and scorn on both sides. He hanged a man suspected of desecrating the American flag, closed a secessionist newspaper and confiscated the property of anyone who would not swear allegiance to the Union. This was part of his first official act as governor, the Federal Confiscation Act. It allowed him to seize the property of any citizen of New Orleans who would not swear loyalty to the Union. But this was not the Butler's greatest crime in the eyes of the entire south... it was Order No. 28.

The women of New Orleans insulted Butler's men in the streets, calling them names and screeching at them. When a woman in the French Quarter opened her window and emptied the contents of a chamber pot over Admiral David Farragut's head, Butler issued General Order Number 28. It simply stated that any woman who insulted a member of the United States Army would be treated from that point as a prostitute, in the midst of plying her trade.

Needless to say, the men and women of the south were outraged and called Butler everything from "unchivalrous" to "Beast". Butler refused to back down and the harassment of his men stopped. Incidentally, no woman was ever arrested. From that point on, the ladies had to resign themselves to hiring artists to paint the likeness of Butler in the bottom of their porcelain chamber pots.

Butler also tore apart two other old New Orleans institutions, a historical landmark and the institution of slavery. The statue of Andrew Jackson had been standing in the city's Jackson Square for six years when the Union troops arrived, honoring the fact that Old Hickory had saved the city from the British in 1815. Butler order these words carved into the pedestal, calculated to enrage the citizens of New Orleans: "The Union must and shall be preserved."

Butler also quickly turned the friction between masters and slaves to the Union's advantage. He declared the plantation owners to be disloyal to the Union and he confiscated their property, in this case, their slaves, and set them free. The freed blacks left the plantations and fled behind Union lines. "I was always a friend of southern rights, " Butler said, "but an enemy of southern wrongs".

The history of Old New Orleans ends with the last shots of the Civil War. The period of Reconstruction in Louisiana is the most tragic time suffered by her people. New Orleans had been the richest city in America and now it became the poorest. The people were stripped of all they had and the commercial business was destroyed. The slave system was now gone and river transportation had been replaced by the railroad. Congress finally re-admitted Louisiana to the Union in June 1868. The period from the end of Reconstruction to the Depression of the 1890's was marked by racial and political upheaval in the city. However, the city of today was built on the ruins of the old ways.

In 1905, New Orleans finally learned to curb the outbreaks of Yellow Fever that had plagued the city since its inception. Until that time, New Orleans had been dependent upon cisterns for drinking water. The cisterns were the breeding places for the mosquitoes that carried the disease. Once a water purification plant was installed, the cisterns were destroyed. Since that time, Yellow Fever has been a thing of the past.

Another long-time enemy of the city was the Mississippi River. Although dependent on the waterway for commerce and transportation, the annual floods wreaked havoc on New Orleans. Each season, the levees were built higher and stronger, but they did little to curb influx of water that came from the spring thaws on the Upper Mississippi. In the 1920's, a spillway was created that shifted much of the water from the river into Lake Pontchartrain, thus eliminating the dangers created by the flooding.

Business and commerce suffered in New Orleans throughout the end of the 1800's and into the early portion of the Twentieth Century. This was mainly because the city did not attract major manufacturing as other southern cities like Atlanta and Baltimore had. The effects of the Civil War continued to be felt until about 1914, when World War I would cause New Orleans would once again be recognized as a major shipping port. This seemed the beginning of a return to brighter days for the region... but troubled times were still ahead.

The Kingfish

As New Orleans passed into the Twentieth Century, the business and cultural climate began to change. The government, which had once been under the control of the state's plantation aristocracy, now passed from the Reconstruction governors to the tutelage of out-of-state corporations. These growing corporations had scooped up the struggling oil, shipping, lumber and sugarcane businesses that had suffered through the late 1800's. By the 1920's, New Orleans was no longer a city controlled by a few wealthy families but it was once again enjoying the development and commerce that had abandoned it years ago. The large companies who had moved in were spreading money throughout the city, building skyscrapers in the downtown area and restoring the battered buildings in the French Quarter.

Of course, this was all fine for those in the city, but this progress was far removed from the blue-collar workers and small farmers in the rest of the state.

In 1929, the Great Depression hit America, spelling catastrophe for many New Orleans banks and businesses. Following close behind the disaster came the voice of change for the desperate times. A former patent medicine salesman from northern Louisiana named Huey P. Long suddenly appeared on the scene and made a bid for the position of governor of the state. Long (who would later be nicknamed "The Kingfish") promised to break the hold that big business had on the wealth of the state and he vowed to see it re-distributed back among the people. In a state where nearly 12 percent of the population was on federal aid, Long's promises found an eager audience!

From the day that Long won office as the railroad commissioner at age 25, he set out to break the back of Standard Oil, the Rockefeller-owned driller who was one of the largest in the state. Long was a revolutionary, but a down-home one, and the people ate it up.

After Long was elected governor in 1928, the state legislature in Baton Rouge came under his control. He used his power to wreak havoc on the New Orleans politicians and newspapers who had opposed him. After serving as governor, he ran for and won a seat in the US Senate. Before leaving for Washington, he fired the legally elected lieutenant governor and replaced him with two designated successors, thus continuing to control the state from Washington. He even convened 11 special sessions of the state legislature, which passed every bill that he proposed. Long was out of control, but his reign was quickly coming to an end.

On September 8, 1935, Huey Long was murdered by a Baton Rouge doctor named Dr. Carl Weiss. The doctor's motive has never been clear and has been speculated about for years. Some maintain that Weiss was being blackmailed by Long. The stories go that the Kingfish planned to reveal that the doctor's wife, who came from a prominent St. Landry Parish family, had black blood.

However, the family of Dr. Weiss, who was killed during the assassination attempt, still maintains that he was not the killer at all. They say that the bodyguards of Huey Long himself killed him in the crossfire of their assassination attempt!

Regardless, it remains another unsolved mystery of the region.

Modern Times in New Orleans

The World War II era finally brought prosperity back to New Orleans. The local shipyards began producing record numbers of PT boats and landing craft for the United States Navy and the port was used frequently as a shipping point for overseas goods. In fact, it was so busy that it became a target for German submarines. They lurked in the dark gulf waters off the mouth of the Mississippi and sank as many as 13 ships in 1942.

After the war, the city began to reap the benefits of the oil boom in the offshore fields in the Gulf. This lasted until the 1980's, when oil prices dropped and many of the drilling companies returned to Texas. Despite the huge drop in revenue, New Orleans quickly recovered and began to recoup its losses through its tourist industry. New Orleans became a destination point for thousands of travelers, all looking for the rollicking times of Bourbon Street, the havoc of Mardi Gras and a place where history and the present day merge almost seamlessly.

Still, there is a depressing side to all of this as well. In spite of the tourists, new casinos and thriving trade, many of the less advantaged citizens of New Orleans still live in almost Third-World conditions. Statistics say that nearly a third of the households make less than $10,000 per year and almost half of the children live in poverty conditions. It is further estimated that just less than half of the 7,000-10,000 homeless people on New Orleans' streets are under the age of 18. With these kinds of numbers to look at, perhaps its not surprising that the city ranks high on the list of American cities when it comes to the number of violent crimes committed each year.

Despite all of that, the spirit of New Orleans remains strong. The city has always weathered its hardships well, from disasters to disease, floods, war, economic pressures, crime and more, and has always managed to come through it with a flair that no other city has. Perhaps that is because of the strange mixture of people and cultures that makes New Orleans so attractively unique.

Part Two: The Haunted History of New Orleans
The People and Culture of New Orleans

The people of New Orleans are as strange and wondrous a mix as the city itself, reveling in their French heritage and their segregation from the mainstream of American culture. They hold a special affinity for such "heroes" as Jean Lafitte and carefully preserve the social, musical and culinary traditions of the past. The melting pot of the city is European,

African and Cuban, creating an unusual blend of style and usually Catholic-based traditions that sometimes puzzle the outsider. While the various groups of immigrants who have come to New Orleans over the years bring their own cultural oddities, they also guarantee that the city will remain the way that it has always been... an exciting place where a conglomeration of traditions are honored and preserved, yet mingled together in such a way that a whole new world is created from it.

The French and Creoles

In the early days of New Orleans, the French Company of the Indies needed to colonize the territory, so they accepted just about any able-bodied volunteers. As Louisiana was known for being a lawless and distant frontier, it was soon realized that no decent folks would want any part of it. So, the eager "volunteers" usually came from French debtor's prisons and houses of correction. Among them were the "working girls" who were given a choice between prison and the New World.

In 1720, an agent of France named Phillipe, Duc d'Orleans, put a stop to the practice of flushing out the unsavory elements of the French prisons and sending them to New Orleans. Of course, this may be why, among modern, upscale residents of the city, you can rarely find anyone who claims an ancestor in New Orleans prior to 1727!

One of the city's preeminent cultures are the Creoles, although this is confusing, as two distinctly separate groups claim the title. White Creoles use the word to describe themselves as people of European colonial ancestry. They are the descendants of the aristocratic families who trace their family tree back to the French and Spanish colonists who came to New Orleans.

The other group who claims the title of Creole is the "mulattos", "quadroons" and Octoroons" - the light-skinned, part African, Catholics. Many of them bear the same surnames as the white Creoles and often can trace their lineage back to the same ancestors.

Both groups use the word to differentiate themselves as people descended from the European colonists and as long-time familial residents of New Orleans. Both are very proud of their heritage and their culture often sets them apart from other residents of the city, just as it did back in the historic years of the city. It has been noted that the word can really refer to anyone of European descent who was born in the colony.

While the Creole are considered the descendants of the first French immigrants, there were others that followed. In the early 1800's, a group of French refugees arrived in the city, fleeing from a slave revolution in Saint-Domingue (Haiti). Many of the cane planters there packed up their families and came to Louisiana. One of them was John James Audubon, the famous naturalist painter, whose mother had been killed in the revolution.

Another group of French settlers arrived around 1814 and they were the followers of Napoleon. When he was exiled to the island of Elba, many of his beaten soldiers sought passage to the newly American city of New Orleans. According to the stories, many of them came in preparation for Napoleon's victorious return to France, which of course, never took place. There are many stories of planned rescues of the emperor, including one involving Jean Lafitte. However, Napoleon did not live long enough after his defeat to come to America.

One of his exiled lieutenants was Pierre Benjamin Buisson, who designed the New Orleans customhouse and later served as the surveyor for the village of Lafayette, which is now the city's Garden District. He is given credit for naming Napoleon Avenue and for streets in the American district that were dubbed after Napoleon's victories in Milan, Austerlitz, Marengo and Constantinople.

The Napoleon House, the bar that stands at the corner of St. Louis and Chartres Streets in the Vieux Carre, was the home of Mayor Nicholas Girod, who offered it as a residence for Bonaparte. Napoleon never made it to New Orleans, but his personal physician, Dr. C.F. Antommarchi, did move into the house and practiced medicine there for 13 years.

The Cajuns

The name "Cajun" comes from the word "Acadian". Acadia was the French Canadian colony founded in 1604 by Samuel de Champlain and now called Nova Scotia. Champlain was joined in 1632 by 300 settlers who were fleeing from religious persecution in France. This colony lived in nearly complete isolation for almost 100 years until the French and Indian War in 1754. After the war, the British demanded the Acadians pledge allegiance to England and give up their Catholic religion. When they refused, they were rounded up separated from their families and deported with whatever belongings they could carry. Many of them were sent back to France; others to the American colonies, where they became indentured servants, and others remained in hiding in Nova Scotia. They would have remained a lost group had not the Spanish invited them to settle in Louisiana. As Catholics and enemies of the British, the Acadians were ideal Louisiana settlers.

By 1768, the first Acadians had traveled and settled deep in the Louisiana bayous, living in the swamps and with the Indians, learning to eat crawfish and alligator and building canoe-like boats called "pirogues". They rebuilt their closed communities and isolated themselves from the urban Creoles in New Orleans, preferring to live in a more relaxed and looser style than their city-dwelling neighbors. The Cajuns were given a wide berth and as their language remained much like the 17th century French of their ancestors, they had little in common with the other local settlers. This feeling of independence and isolation is what made their culture so different and it remains separate even today.

The Africans

Since the middle 1700's, the culture of the African Americans in New Orleans has been a more powerful driving force than in perhaps any other great American city. The first Africans to come to Louisiana came as slaves in 1719. They had been taken from the Senegambia region of Africa by French slavers and they would be but the first of many. Between the years of 1719 and 1731, the French Company of the Indies was believed to have imported more than 7,000 slaves to the region.

The city of New Orleans quickly set itself apart from other southern cities. In 1727, the city adopted the "Code Noir", a set of rules for the proper treatment of slaves, making the region a less oppressive place for blacks to live than in some areas dominated (at that time) by the British.

The importing of slaves into the United States was outlawed in 1808, but New Orleans was exempted from this law until 1812. Slavery continued until the Civil War and slave auctions were frequently held in the city. During these sales, auctioneers would dress the slaves up in European clothing to make them appear "less fearsome". Slave auction sites included the Cabildo, the St. Louis and St. Charles Hotels and Maspero's Exchange, now a restaurant on Chartres Street.

Early records show that as early as 1805, Congo Square (now Louis Armstrong Park) was a grassy area on the edge of the swamp and just outside of the French Quarter. It became a place where slaves were allowed to congregate and gather for religious rituals and ceremonies. Their African customs were kept alive in this way and many people from various tribal groups discovered a common bond through music and dance. A few years later, the immigration of slaves and former slaves from Haiti served to introduce new tribal customs to the Louisiana slaves.

But not all of the Africans living in New Orleans were slaves. There were many free blacks who were either former slaves or free black immigrants from the Caribbean. Between 1840 and 1860, census records show that there were over 7,500 free blacks in the city and the initials F.P.C. (Free Person of Color) came to be used after the name of a person of mixed race who might be mistaken for white. As oppressive as this was though, New Orleans offered free blacks more rights than any other American city, allowing them to own property and to seek justice in the courts.

There was another aspect of free black life in New Orleans that has become something of a legend. This legend revolves around the "Quadroon Balls" that were once held in what is now a restored meeting room of the Bourbon Orleans Hotel. The Quadroon Ballroom and the

Negro Sisters of the Holy Family's orphanage chapel were once both located here at 717 Orleans Street. Originally located here had been the Orleans Theatre and the Orleans Ballroom, which were destroyed by fire in 1816. John Davis rebuilt the Ballroom in 1817 and it was here that the famous balls were held.

During these extravagant events, mulatto daughters were presented by their mothers as potential mistresses to masked white Creole men. The wealthy sons of business and plantation owners sometimes supported quadroon mistresses and families in addition to their "legitimate" white families. Many have assumed these young women to be no better than prostitutes, but this was not the case. The girls were raised to be proper young women and were as well educated as the times allowed. They were free women and known for their beauty.

After being presented at a ball, the young woman left with a suitable "protector", usually a young Creole gentlemen with money, who would then support her in fitting style. The women would own property in a small house in the upper quarter and often these arrangements would last for many years, or perhaps for life. Most of them became renowned for their successful businesses and rooming houses and were usually well thought of by their neighbors. They were never allowed to marry their white lovers though, which must have left many, both women and men, heart-broken and saddened by what could have been.

The Quadroon Balls lasted for many years, although since they officially did not exist, little record remains as to what exactly occurred during them. Regardless, they were a principal diversion for white men in those days and many would gather here to drink, talk, and hopefully make the acquaintance of one of the beautiful young women.

The balls finally came to an end in the early 1860's and in 1874, a free man of color named Thomas Lafon bought the ballroom for an order of black nuns, the Negro Sisters of the Holy Family. The daughter of a Quadroon mistress had founded the order in New Orleans in 1842. For years, the old ballroom was an assembly room for the convent's orphanage until later becoming a part of the hotel that stands on the site today.

The Civil War, and most particularly Lincoln's Emancipation Proclamation of January 1, 1863, ended the institution of slavery in the southern states... except in New Orleans. Because the city had the bad luck to be under federal control at the time, slavery would last longer here than in any other place in the United States. In fact, it was allowed to continue for almost a year by the federal occupation forces.

Once freed, the slaves now discovered that they had nowhere to go. They were shunned by the whites and ostracized by the free people of color. These newly freed people were poor, uneducated and usually darker-skinned than the already free blacks. Raised on American plantations, they also spoke only English, which hampered them ever further. Most of the former slaves moved into a poor area of the city called "Back-a-Town". Although little more than a slum, it still managed to produce notables like Louis Armstrong and Mahalia Jackson.

The period of Reconstruction was a terrible time for the free people of color in New Orleans. The most wealthy of them, many who owned slaves themselves, lived in relative seclusion in the Seventh Ward downtown. They were French-speaking professionals who educated their children in France and among them were master craftsmen and the creators of Jazz. When Reconstruction came however, they found themselves stripped of the freedoms and wealth they had once enjoyed. Disgusted with what the city had become, many of them left and immigrated to Latin America and Europe. Others moved into uptown neighborhoods, married recent immigrants and if light-skinned enough, permanently crossed over the line from black to white.

The Other Europeans

The Spanish are sometimes referred to (only half in jest) as New Orleans' first tourists. While the Spanish rule of Louisiana only lasted for 34 years, from 1769-1803, the city was permanently influenced by not only Spanish culture and architecture, but also by the Spanish settlements in Texas, Florida and the Caribbean.

Spanish rule was never pleasantly accepted by the French settlers and more than once, military force was needed to sooth the unrest. More drastic steps were taken when Spanish governors even married members of the local French aristocracy in hopes of avoiding further outbreaks of violence. Governor Luis de Unzaga married the first French bride and a few years later, the third Spanish governor, Don Bernardo de Galvez, wed Felicie d'Estrehan, a popular first lady of Louisiana.

Galvez also became an integral part of the American Revolution in the south. During his eight-year administration from 1777 to 1785, he supplied the American frontiersmen with weapons and seized every British ship that he could. He also organized armies to capture Baton Rouge, Natchez, Mobile and Pensacola, earning the gratitude of the new government after the war.

The fourth governor, Miro, also took a local bride, the wealthy Celeste Eleanor Elizabeth Macarty, the daughter of a leading Irish Creole family. Her father and uncle had come to New Orleans in 1731 as part of a French marine detachment and had stayed on. Bienville had honored the two men as "Chevaliers de Saint Louis" and had assisted them in getting large land grants.

The Spanish influence in the city has remained strong over the years, thanks in large part to the restoration of the Vieux Carre after the great fire in 1788. The Latin influence grew once again in the mid-1900's when political upheavals in Latin America and Cuba bought many new immigrants to the city.

The Germans are perhaps the most overlooked immigrants in the history of New

Orleans, although there is no question that their presence was imperative to the survival of the early colony. Shortly after the arrival of the first settlers in Louisiana, John Law's Company of the Indies came to the conclusion that unless they could find farmers to work the land, the French colonists would have nothing to eat. With this in mind, they began advertising in southern Germany and Switzerland for farmers to come to the New World. The Louisiana colony was billed as a "paradise", a poor description of the land at that time, being as it was a poorly drained swamp that was infested with disease.

The first large group of German Catholics set sail from France in 1719 and shortly after they left port, a cholera epidemic broke out. Once they arrived, this bad news was met with more dismal information. They so learned that New Orleans, the so-called "Paris of the New World", was far from the perfect place to live. Not long after, John Law's scheme failed and he fled to Italy, leaving the German farmers stranded in French-speaking Louisiana. Law had promised the Germans both money and land and they were still waiting for both when they learned that their new homeland was now a possession of Spain. The Germans quickly abandoned New Orleans and moved 25 miles upriver to a place that became known as the "German Coast".

Here, they found an area much better suited to farming and began supplying the city with an abundance of grain, vegetables and produce. And not only were they excellent farmers, but they also gained a reputation as fine bakers of French bread and pastries as well. Even today, most of the top New Orleans bakeries bear Swiss and German family names.

More Germans came to New Orleans during the great waves of European immigration in the last 1800's and early 1900's. Their industrious nature made them successful in business and in commercial beer brewing and their musical styles quickly found a place with the upbeat tempos of New Orleans' famous marching bands.

If the Germans were the most overlooked of the New Orleans immigrants, then the Irish were the most unappreciated. From the very beginnings of the colony, New Orleans proved an attractive destination to Irish Catholics who shared a common enemy in England with both the French and the Spanish. Many of them found their way to New Orleans through military service with both countries. Once there, they tended to marry into the Creole families and adapt their last names accordingly. For instance, the builder of the Gallier House, which is now a museum in the French Quarter, was originally an Irishman named Gallagher.

The early arrival Irish Creoles (known as the "lace curtain Irish") differed greatly from the Irish immigrants who came later, mainly during the great potato famine of the middle 1800's. In the years after the 1845 potato blight, hundreds of thousands of poor and starving Irish immigrants came through the port of New Orleans. They arrived in a city where nearly all of the useful land had already claimed, where little housing could be found and where slaves did all of the menial labor. The new arrivals were unable to afford passage to the northern cities and so they became stranded in a city where they simply weren't needed.

These immigrants could often be hired for next to nothing and were considered useful labor for jobs that were considered too dangerous for a servant or a slave. One of these tasks was to dig the city's canal systems. The Irish laborers took to the job and managed to survive both the brutal work and the bouts of Yellow Fever that came with digging and living in the swamps.

In such a way, the Irish left an indelible mark on the city and on America in general. The first statue ever erected in honor of a woman in the United States was dedicated to an illiterate Irish immigrant named Margaret Haughery. She is credited for caring for hundreds of Irish children who were orphaned after the Yellow Fever epidemics. Her statue stands in a small park at Camp and Prytania with an inscription that reads simply "Margaret".

The Italians began to arrive in New Orleans during the 1700's, attracted by the Latin and Catholic culture of the region. As with the Irish, many of the aristocratic Italians came to the region in military service with France or Spain. Far greater numbers came later, part of the last great wave of immigrants to New Orleans in the late 1800's. By 1890, there were more than 15,000 Italians living in the city, mostly in the crumbling French Quarter, which had fallen out of favor with most Creole families. Outside of New York, New Orleans saw more Italian immigrants than anywhere else in America did and the majority of them came from Sicily.

The late-coming Italians were treated just a little worse than the Irish, but better than the blacks, but like these groups, the Italians managed to survive. Two of the most notable of these immigrants were Joseph Vacarro and Mother Frances Xavier Cabrini. Vacarro started out as a door-to-door fruit peddler but later went on to found the Standard Fruit and Steamship Company, while Mother Cabrini became the first American citizen to be canonized by the Catholic Church. She came to New Orleans in 1892 as a missionary to the French Quarter, which was nearly 90 percent Italian by that time. Within her lifetime, she established nearly 70 different institutions to aid immigrants to the city, including hospitals, orphanages and even St. Mary's Italian Church, which became a focal point for the lives of French Quarter residents.

During the 1970's, four of New Orleans' seven city councilmen, as well as the mayor and the chief of police, were of Italian heritage. Even today, a visit to vegetable stalls in the French market, grocery stores in the French Quarter, ice cream shops or some of the excellent local restaurants will confirm that the Italian culture continues to thrive in the city.

Other facets of the Sicilian culture have left as mark on the city as well, as we will discover in the next chapter.

A Taste of New Orleans - Food & Music in the Big Easy

There are several things that truly define the spirit of New Orleans but three of the most important are probably the food, the music and, of course, the ghosts. The food in New Orleans is as wonderfully mixed as the culture of the city itself. The local restaurants here are

Some of New Orleans' Most Famous Fare

ANDOUILLE: A Fat and spicy country sausage that is often used in jambalaya and gumbo and to accompany a big plate of red beans and rice.

BEIGNET: Beignets are like little square doughnuts that are served hot and sprinkled with powdered sugar. They are addictive and best eaten after midnight at Cafe du Monde, located near Jackson Square. This 24-hour a day cafe serves both tourist and local alike and you can see a little bit of EVERYTHING while seated at one of the outdoor tables.

CAFE' AU LAIT: Chicory coffee that is served with steamed milk. Chicory is a root that is dried, roasted and ground and produces a thick, syrupy coffee. It's considered a delicacy in New Orleans.

CRAWFISH: Affectionately known as "mudbugs", these tiny lobster-like creatures are plentiful in the local waters and are eaten in every conceivable way.

DIRTY RICE: Rice cooked with chicken livers and gizzards, onions, chopped celery, peppers and chicken stock.

DRESSED: While not actually a dish, it's helpful to know what this means when ordering a sandwich in New Orleans. It means that you want it "with the works".

ETOUFEE': A spicy shrimp and crawfish stew that is served over rise. It means "smothered" in French

FILE': A thickener that is made from ground sassafras leaves. It is usually used to thicken gumbo.

known for their delectable Creole and Cajun dishes, which oddly did not come from French cooking, but from a combination of both native and imported styles.

The early settlers to New Orleans did not bring with them any particular dish and in fact, would have starved to death long before they could invent one. Luckily, the native Indian population was willing to share with them the secrets of eating in the inhospitable land. They introduced the French to a variety of breads and mushy cereals made from corn, dried beans and different kinds of squash that all still popular today. In addition, they taught them of syrups and berries that could be used to flavor meat and how to thicken stews using sassafras, or file' powder, as it is called today.

Despite this new-found abundance of food, the settlers still yearned for the foods they had at home and what they missed the most was bread. Unfortunately, the area around New Orleans was too wet to grow wheat. Many of the wealthier residents had grown used to accomplished chefs and servants back home, but the majority of the settlers were peasants, convicts and prostitutes and, except for the lack of bread, were satisfied to dine on whatever they could find.

It would be the Ursuline Sisters who would bring French culinary skills to New Orleans. A condition of their contract with the Company of the Indies stated that they would cultivate an herb garden in the city, which they did. They were then able to teach the benefits of using bay leaves in stews and soups and in using the plants for medicinal purposes.

While the Ursulines were teaching the rudiments of French cuisine to the settlers, the African slaves were busy creating their own fare, making the best foods they could from what they had to work with. Many of these black cooks had come from an ancient African culinary tradition and the stories say that many of them were descended from ancestors who had traded with the Arab spice merchants as far back as the 11th century. They began creating the stews and gumbos that have become staples of New Orleans cuisine.

As time passed, a good cook became crucial to one's social standing in New Orleans. A Creole lady never ventured far from the kitchen when an important meal was being prepared. Many kitchen slaves were even taught to read so that they could adapt French recipes into New Orleans fare. The black cooks used the French peasant's thickener, the "roux", and turned it into a dark base that is used for many local specialties like etouffee, gumbo, Creole sauce and turtle soup.

The Spanish brought their own culinary customs to New Orleans, along with ideas adapted from the Mayans and the Aztecs of Central America. Centuries before, Columbus had brought yams, kidney beans, maize, red peppers and allspice back to Europe and other explorers later brought the tomato from Mexico. The Spaniards then reintroduced the pepper and the tomato back to the New World in Louisiana and began adding green peppers to sauces and meat dishes, mostly to keep them from spoiling. The tomato, when mixed with the roux, became an important part of Shrimp Creole. The Spanish dish called "paella", made from rice and shellfish, became the Creole dish "jambalaya" when ham was added to it.

GUMBO: A thick, spicy soup that is prepared with just about anything, but always includes rice. You can find anything in the mix from seafood to chicken to alligator to andouille sausage. To illustrate the fine points of gumbo, there is a New Orleans legend about a Creole man who dies and went to heaven. When he arrived at the pearly gates, he told St. Peter that he intended to have a bowl of gumbo. He was informed that there was no gumbo in heaven, that spicy foods were not allowed there, that heaven was the land of milk and honey. Needless to say, the Creole man decided to go to hell instead... where the partaking of spicy gumbo was not a sin!

HUSH PUPPIES: Fried balls of cornmeal, often served as a side dish to seafood.

JAMBALAYA: A traditional Cajun rice dish that typically includes tomatoes, shrimp, ham, onions and just about anything the cook wants to include.

LAGNIAPPE: A little something extra that comes free with your order.

MUFFULETTA: Round, Italian bread that is filled with an assortment of cold cuts, cheese and olive salad. These sandwiches are normally huge and best shared with friends.

PAIN PERDU: Literally translated as "lost bread", this is a wonderful local version of French Toast that is made with French bread.

PO BOYS: Sandwiches that are similar to submarines but with rich French bread and tons of ingredients. Served both hot and cold.

PRALINES: A sweet confection made from brown sugar and pecans. You will NOT be able to east just one of these addictive treats!

TASSO: A smoked and spicy Cajun ham.

The waves of European immigration brought other flavors and additions to the Creole style. Aristocrats fleeing the French Revolution brought innovations on haute cuisine. Plantation owners and free people of color brought fish dishes with Spanish spices from the West Indies. Sicilians brought pastas and rich sauces from Europe. All of these arrivals created dishes that are still enjoyed today like pain perdu (a local French toast), red beans and rice, Cajun boudin sausage, gumbo, bread pudding and chicory cafe' au lait.

The Civil War brought a great change to the household economy of the Creoles and while their economic status floundered, they continued to enjoy eating and entertaining. Rich foods and meats were replaced with simpler gumbos made from fresh vegetable and what little meat they could spare. When the price of ice was beyond their means, they would crush glass and sew it into cheesecloth bags. The tinkling sound as it floated in pitchers provided the illusion of ice and if the guests even noticed, they didn't care. Most of them knew they might be hosting a dinner under the same circumstances the following week. This sort of hospitality and pride has managed to preserve the Creole cuisine through the years.

Ironically, the influx of tourists into New Orleans in the 1960's and 1970's, which revived the local economy, came close to destroying the long-held culinary traditions of the city. As most Americans of this time period favored bland, simple foods, many of the local hotels and restaurants were forced to create an "Americanized" version of New Orleans favorites. Chicory was taken out of the coffee, file' powder was rarely used, crabs and oysters were removed from the gumbo and black peppers replaced the cayenne pepper in every dish. Creole cooking was banished from the restaurants and remained alive only in homes and in a few of the diehard local establishments.

Finally, by the late 1980's, food lovers were hungry again for spicy flavors and more daring fare. The Creole and Cajun cuisines once again appeared and became a major drawing card for the city. Travelers came from all over to sample foods that remain unique to the Crescent City. To eat a meal in New Orleans today is to immerse yourself in culture, flavor and history and to become just a small part of a tradition that stretches back to the beginning of the city itself.

Jazz is one of America's only real indigenous art forms and if there is a spiritual birthplace for this incredible music, it is Old Congo Square, which is now Louis Armstrong Park in New Orleans. Here, the African slaves who were brought to the city were allowed to meet, dance and play their traditional instruments. This continued for many years, until about 1857, but after the Civil War, bands like Kelly's Silver Coronet Band performed there. These were times when the melodies of slave work chants and the blues mingled and in the early 1900's, the buoyant, simple music became known as "traditional" jazz.

During these early years, white musicians began to hang out on the street or in the clubs, trying to learn the style of the black musical community. They adopted their own style of jazz, which became known as "Dixieland". The jazz music played by the African-American community was more improvisational than Dixieland and found its roots in African and West Indian traditions.

The word "jazz" would not be applied to the new sound until almost 20 years after it captured the hearts of New Orleans audiences though. They referred to the music in more visceral terms like "gutbucket", "ragtime" or "ratty music". Despite being created by African musicians, it is believed that a white group was the first to be called a "jazz band". In 1915, Tom Brown took his white Dixieland band to Chicago, where it was met with delight by northern audiences. Other Chicago musicians were not so fond of it though and angrily used "jass" as a slur for musicians who played that "dirty New Orleans music". Chicago enthusiasts knew something good when they heard it and started calling the group "Brown's Dixieland Jass Band".

Legends of New Orleans also cite another area as the birthplace of jazz, the brothels of the infamous Storyville District. Outdoor performances in this area by performers like Jelly Roll Morton and Louis Armstrong created a wide audience for jazz and the brothels provided steady work for pianists who could play a catchy tune.

Jelly Roll Morton, who had been born Ferdinand Joseph La Mothe, insisted that he had been the creator of jazz. While this statement may not have been completely accurate, there is no denying that he was the first notable jazz composer and arranger. As a Creole of color, he felt himself intellectually superior to most musicians and was known for being a flashy dresser and ladies man, as well as an expert pool hustler. Morton also possessed a terrific fear of the power of voodoo and it was said that he was known for throwing away a perfectly good suit of clothes if he thought that someone had thrown "voodoo powder" on him.

The name of Louis Armstrong will forever be connected to New Orleans jazz. The charismatic performer got his earliest musical training on the streets and as a ward of the Jones Colored Waif's Home. He began playing professionally in the early 1900's and by 1918 was playing on the riverboats. In 1922, he left New Orleans for Chicago and spent the next 40 years performing around the world.

Another traditionally New Orleans form of jazz is the street parade that goes back well over a century to the first jazz funerals. They began with jazz musicians who performed whenever one of their brethren died and have since gone on to become a popular form of local entertainment.

In the jazz funeral parade, the band follows the coffin and behind that it the second line, made up of family, friends and mourners. On the way to the grave, the mood is somber and the music played is a slow dirge that is accompanied by a muffled drum. On the walk home however, jubilation and rejoicing overtakes the group as they celebrate the departed's joyful entry into heaven and the music becomes much more upbeat and happy.

Jazz funeral parades today can be hired to play at both funerals and parades and still donate their time for the services of fellow musicians.

During the 1940's, as music on the radio became more popular, a demand began to grow for a big-city sound in New Orleans. The term "rhythm and blues" was coined in the magazine "Variety" as a category for its hit charts but in New Orleans, the musicians put their own spin on the music they heard. They added their own unique soul and jazz to it and fused it into their own version of "rhythm and blues". One of the most popular locations for this new sound was a placed called The Dew Drop Inn. The club featured blues players like Gatemouth Brown and Big Joe Turner, big jazz bands like Lionel Hampton and Duke Ellington and local performers like Allen Touissant, Charles Neville and Guitar Slim. The club no longer exists today, but the sound it created has never been forgotten.

In 1949, a former tap dancer and blues pianist named Henry Roeland Byrd took the professional name of "Professor Longhair" and created a wild musical blend of mambo, calypso, blues and jazz. Until his death in 1980, he had a profound effect on the younger musicians who followed like Fats Domino and a white pianist named Mac Rebenneck. In 1968, Rebenneck hit it big as "Dr. John", a name he took from a famous Voodoo priest of the 1800's.

In the 1960's, a Creole of color named Allen Toussaint began to nurture the talents of many local artists like Aaron Neville, who later joined with his brothers to form the legendary Neville Brothers, the Dixie Cups, Ernie K-Doe, Lee Dorsey and Irma Thomas.

In the 1980's, New Orleans music became popular again as two former students of the New Orleans Center for the Creative Arts won Grammy Awards while they were still in their twenties. They were Wynton Marsalis, the son of noted jazz pianist, teacher and trumpet player Terence Blanchard and Harry Connick, Jr., whose father is a local district attorney and musical performer.

The other most famous forms of local music are Cajun and Zydeco, both rollicking and entertaining blends of accordions, homemade percussion, and the French language. The music stems from the French ballads that the first Acadian settlers brought with them from Nova Scotia. A generation later, German farmers added the accordion to the mix, creating a generally upbeat and joyful sound.

Cajun music is characterized by the inclusion of the fiddle and hand-held triangle while Zydeco combines African blues with traditional Cajun dance music. Both of them manage to create a sound that is distinctly New Orleans and ultimately unforgettable.

Carnival and Mardi Gras

Another (huge) part of New Orleans culture is Mardi Gras. In many Catholic dominated cities around the world, the days prior to Easter are called Lent, a period of fasting and penitence. Lent begins with Ash Wednesday, which reminds believers of their own mortality but in New Orleans, the Tuesday before Lent is Mardi Gras, which literally means "Fat Tuesday". It is considered the last gasp of frivolity before a period of austerity.

In New Orleans, the term "Carnival" refers to the season of balls and parades that begins on Twelfth Night and continues through Mardi Gras. On that day, one "krewe" (a club that holds a parade, a ball, or both) hosts the first ball of the season. The high point of Carnival is the parade -filled, 4-day weekend that begins on the Saturday before Ash Wednesday and ends in an all-out bash on Mardi Gras day.

Mardi Gras was celebrated in Christian countries long before the founding of New Orleans. The day that the French explorers camped below New Orleans in 1699 happened to be Mardi Gras, March 3, so they named the place Pointe du Mardi Gras. It wasn't long before the French began celebrating the holiday in Louisiana and historians have found record of masked balls and street processions in New Orleans from the early 1700's.

Officials were already clamping down on the fun by 1791 with a statement that declared Mardi Gras was a public hazard and gave "people of color, both free and slave, to take advantage of carnival, going about disguised, mingling with the throngs in the streets, seeking entrance to masquerade balls, and threatening public peace." By 1806, the party had become so rowdy that the celebration was outright forbidden. However, this became a law that was summarily ignored. In 1817, another pointless proclamation was passed, this time banning masks. By 1823, the authorities must have realized that to ban Mardi Gras was futile, so the celebration once again became legal. Three years later, masks were once again allowed.

In the 1800's, balls became very popular, so popular in fact that another law was passed that limited the season from January 1 through Mardi Gras Day. This was done, so the records say, to keep people from celebrating all year long. In 1837, the season was lengthened from November 1 to June 1.

Another, integral part of the celebration are the parades, of which there are many during the carnival. There has been much debate as to whether the first parade was held in 1835 or 1838, but regardless, the early parades (like today) were described as "wicked".

The flair employed today by the old krewes has it roots in the celebrations planned in 1872 when the Russian Grand Duke Alexis Romanoff came to New Orleans at carnival time. He came to the city in pursuit of the stage actress Lydia Thompson but the people of New Orleans planned marvelous entertainment for him anyway. Forty businessmen got together and founded the Krewe of Rex, launching a daytime parade in the Grand Duke's honor. The upper-crust members of New Orleans society decided to adopt the Romanoff household colors of purple, green and gold as the official colors of the Carnival. They also learned that the Grand Duke's favorite song was a ditty called "If Ever I Cease to Love You" from the New York musical "Bluebeard" that starred Lydia Thompson. After all of these years, the forgettable tune remains the official song of Carnival.

And thus ends our journey into the historical side of New Orleans. From here, we begin our descent into the darker side of the region.... a side that evokes images of death, murder, sin, corruption, and finally, ghosts.

Prepare yourself, because things are going to get a little bumpy during the ride ahead!

Amy Taylor in Jackson Square

Chapter Two
Sin & The City
The Dark Side of New Orleans

The city of New Orleans has long been a breeding ground for just about every assortment of pleasure and vice. For many decades, people have come here to laugh, drink, and enjoy themselves for the city is known for showing her visitors a very good time. The more virtuous among us might call the place a "den of iniquity", drenched in wickedness and sin. To this, a typical resident of the Crescent City would reply that life is meant to be lived.

But for all of the good times and parties and the harmless sins, there is a darker side to the city.. a side that can make grown men weep and those of the faint of heart to cower in fear.

One of the Famous Houses of Storyville

The Bright Lights of Storyville

For many years, one of the most popular attractions in New Orleans was the "Red Light District" that was located off Basin Street. There was no other collection of brothels in America that was quite like it and the legends said that you could find "everything" in this area, from mansion-like establishments with mirrored ceilings, fine wines and caviar where one night with a young woman might cost $50, to the individual prostitute who carried a carpet on her back and might charge you two bits. It was said that 1,000 to 2,000 women plied the world's oldest profession in this district and that many times that number lived off the business, collecting rent, serving food and drink and playing music.

The area around Basin Street was all legal and above-board too. Prostitution was a welcome tradition in New Orleans from the very beginning. Some of the first female settlers to come to the city were the French prostitutes who had been given the choice between Louisiana and prison. In 1744, a French officer was said to comment that "there were not 10 women of blameless character in the entire city". Whether this was meant as a criticism or a compliment is unknown, but New Orleans maintained a reputation for being able to offer visiting sailors a large supply of informal companions for the evening. What kind of port would it be if working girls were not readily available to mariners after months at sea or to frontiersmen who braved the Mississippi on the flatboats?

As the more prudish Americans took over New Orleans in 1803, they attempted to clean up the bawdy atmosphere of the city. At this point, prostitution was prohibited on the ground floors of any building and the working women were no longer allowed to go out looking for customers. They now had to remain in one location and let the customers look for them. In the 1840's, a number of astute businessmen arranged with city officials to allow brothels to be located near the city's big hotels, the St. Louis and the St. Charles, so that visitors wouldn't have to go far to find a little welcoming companionship.

By 1857, the madams and their girls were required to obtain licenses to operate in the city. If the madam paid $250 per year and each of her girls $100, they could operate anywhere above the first floor of the house and in some parts of the city, on the first floor as well. The mayor personally administered this licensing system.

By this time, certain political officials began to toy with the idea of a restricted area for prostitution and many had their eyes on Basin Street, a small thoroughfare that ran alongside Rampart Street on the far edge of the French Quarter. Not long after, a number of three-storied mansions appeared here and wagons brought heavy furniture, expensive decorations, mirrors and fine rugs to their doors. These furnishings were followed by thoroughly "painted women" and their stables of young girls.

When a few of the local residents complained about the newcomers, they found that their protests fell on deaf ears. This was especially true after the beginning of the Civil War, when the Basin Street area became popular with the occupying Federal troops. The cluster of bawdy houses stayed busy after the war as well and attracted well-known madams like Hattie Hamilton, Kate Townsend, "Countess" Willie Piazza and Josie Arlington, New Orleans' favorite madam.

The house operated by Josie Arlington opened in the 1870's and was a posh and decorous mansion that catered to the finest men in the city. The house was filled with original oil paintings, statuary and potted palms. It was staffed by the madam's most stunning quadroon and octoroon "nieces", who were usually girls whose families had fallen on hard times.

Unfortunately, Basin Street was not the only place in the city where brothels were beginning to appear and things began to get out of hand. In 1897, Alderman Sidney Story, a respected businessman, proposed an ordinance to rid the residential neighborhoods of the bawdy houses and confine them to a single district. The proposed area became a 38-square section around Basin Street, which ironically came to be called "Storyville". Despite his protests, the area was dubbed with the alderman's name and would forever be remembered that way.

Most of the non-professional folks moved out of the area and for blocks, new businesses came into being as cafes, saloons, flop-houses, gambling halls and anything else that could take advantage of the notoriety of the district opened up. Thousands of people began to share in the business in one way or another, creating a rather booming economy based on vice.

Basin Street itself has the finest of the houses. Here, carriages drew up to hitching posts and doormen in livery ushered gentlemen into the establishments. In several of the places, a caller would feel out of place if not in evening attire, as he would find the girls in ballroom gowns awaiting selection. Drinks could be ordered at steep prices of $5 for bottles of champagne and as much as $1 for beer. Many of the gaudier houses also installed new electric lights and stained glass windows to go along with the elaborate decor.

From all over, women flocked to Storyville. Appealing to local pride though, a few madams gave preference to local girls, hoping to provide employment to "talented" natives. One house advertised that they had recently acquired women of "royal blood" who were traveling incognito. The competitors laughed and claimed the "noble" young women were can-can dancers from Philadelphia or New York. One house presented a "Lady Estelle" who wore a mask when working because of her fear of being discovered. A customer who recognized a mole however, exposed her as Maggie Johansen, who had been charging $2 at a house down the street the year before!

But this did not deter the men who came. They were paying, and gladly, for an illusion. It was a need that the madams catered to with engraved cards, letters and merchandise lists that were sent to businessmen and politicians around town.

But not all of the houses, or the girls who inhabited them, were so graceful. Alongside the fancy mansions were the middle range houses and of course, those that were three rungs lower. On side streets, especially along Franklin and St. Louis, were the one-storied wooden cribs. They were rows of single rooms in each of which waited a bureau, a bed and a woman. From these places, the women could be seen leaning out and calling from the window to the men on the street. In the alleys here, a man who strolled by risked not only his belongings but also his life. A half-dozen women were liable to appear and snatch at his hand, each trying to pull him into their room. One might grab his hat, forcing him to follow her to get it back. Many of the men were drugged or knocked over the head and would awaken later to find their pockets picked.

Most of the time though, crime of this sort was not tolerated in Storyville. For many years, the central authority in the district was Tom Anderson, dubbed the "second Mayor" of New Orleans. He was a member of the state legislature who owned several saloons in Storyville and who handled business matters in the area. He watched over things and made sure that things operated smoothly, from making sure customers were happy to insuring that the proper protection money was being paid for the larger houses. He entertained many eminent sightseers to Storyville like John L. Sullivan, "Gentleman Jim" Corbett, and others and made sure they enjoyed themselves.

But Storyville was never meant to last. At the beginning of World War I, the Secretary of the Navy, Josephus "Tea Totaling" Daniels, threatened to close down the New Orleans Naval Base if Storyville was not shut down. The district was officially closed in 1917 and prostitution once again became a clandestine activity. It was the end of an era in New Orleans.

For years after, the brothels of Storyville silently deteriorated along Basin Street. They were the dim ghosts of memory past. Then, in the 1930's, most of the district was lost forever when Storyville was demolished to make way for the Iberville Housing Project.

The Mafia in New Orleans

One of the most notorious crimes in New Orleans history involved the 1890 assassination of David C. M. Hennessey, the first superintendent of the New Orleans Police Department. Accused of the crime were 19 members of a Sicilian gang and although acquitted of any wrongdoing, 11 of them were later lynched by a mob.

New Orleans at that time was probably the most anti-Italian city in America. The city had recently been flooded with thousands of Italian immigrants and statements from the Mayor's office didn't help matters any. In one letter, Mayor Joseph A. Shakespeare called Southern Italians and Sicilians ".... the most idle, vicious and worthless people among us."

Of course, not all of the blame could be laid at city government's door either. In addition to dirty politicians and cops on the take, late 1800's New Orleans was also filled with Italian criminals. There was no denying that the French Quarter ghetto was turning out productive Italian citizens, but it was also turning out criminals as well. Undoubtedly, many of these criminals were not "mafiosi", but it has long been conceded that New Orleans represented one of the main ports of entry for the Mafia into the United States.

No one really knows when the first appearance of the Mafia in America took place but experts believe that it was in New Orleans in the late 1800's. Between 1888 and 1890, the New Orleans Mafia, made up of several Sicilian groups, committed an estimated 40 murders without opposition. During this period, Antonio and Carlo Matranga took control of the Mississippi River docks. Tribute had to be paid to them before a freighter could be unloaded. Soon, the Provenzano brothers, leaders of another Mafia group, challenged their operation. War broke out between the two gangs and killings on the docks became regular occurrences.

The police failed to stop the battles until the chief of police, David Hennessey, personally took over the case. Soon, the Matrangas began to find themselves investigated and harassed at every turn, while the Provenzanos were not bothered at all.

Slain Police Chief David Hennessey

The Matrangas sent a warning to the chief, but the pressure continued. At this point, they tried to bribe him, but he turned them down, leading them to believe the Provenzanos were simply paying him more. So they fell back onto an old Sicilian custom of killing a government official who got in the way.

Hennessey became a marked man when police, conducting a routine murder investigation, charged two Provenzano brothers with the murder of a Matranga gangster whose head had been cut off and stuffed in a fireplace. The Matrangas, determined to thwart the Provenzano operations, hired some of the city's best attorneys to aid in the prosecution. Then, Chief Hennessey made a startling statement to the newspapers... he told them that he had uncovered the existence of a criminal society, the Mafia, in New Orleans and he would offer proof during the Provenzano trial.

On October 15, 1890, Hennessey left his office for home but was cut down by a shotgun blast less than a half-block from his house. Hennessey managed to fire a few volleys at his fleeing assailants and when asked who shot him, he whispered "Dagoes", then died.

The murder outraged the citizens of New Orleans. A grand jury was convened and they announced that the existence of the Mafia in the city had now been established beyond doubt.

They chose 19 men who they believed were not only members of the Mafia, but also involved in the murder of Chief Hennessey. A trial was held, but was believed by most to be a farce. Not only were a large number of the 60 witnesses threatened and paid off, but members of the jury were bribed too. Despite what was regarded as overwhelming evidence against at least 11 of the defendants, all but three were acquitted and the jury was unable to reach a verdict on those three.

All of the defendants were returned to the parish prison to await final disposition of their cases and what followed was a blight on the history of New Orleans. During the two nights following the trial, mass meetings and protests were held in the city. Finally, a mob of several thousand, headed by at least 60 leading citizens, marched on the prison. They had a "death list" of the 11 defendants against whom the evidence had been the strongest.

Two of the mafiosi were pulled screaming from their cells and were hanged from lampposts. Seven others were executed by firing squad in the prison yard while two more were shot to death when they ran and hid in the kennel belonging to the jail's guard dog.

While some newspapers denounced the murders, the citizens and especially the business community seemed rather pleased about what had occurred. A new song "Hennessey Avenged" made the rounds and became quite popular.

For a short time, the killings threatened international relations. Italy recalled its ambassador and severed diplomatic relations with the United States. The government demanded reparations and punishment against the leaders of the lynch mob. Eventually, the affair was settled when Washington paid $25,000 to the men's relatives in Italy.

The murders did not end the presence of the Mafia in New Orleans however, despite what newspapers of the time would have the reader believe. They did leave an impression on the local mafiosi though. Carlo Matranga, who took over leadership of the Mafia in New Orleans until the early 1920's, took a place in the background and issued orders that were carried out by front men. This would remain a tradition through modern times and rarely would anything illegal be pinned on local crime bosses.

Perhaps the most notorious of these crime bosses was Carlos "Little Man" Marcello. Born in 1910, Marcello came to Louisiana as a baby. His family settled in Algiers, the community across the river from New Orleans, and he started out as a small-time hood. By the 1940's, he had moved into the big business, when he went to work for New York gangster Frank Costello in the slot machine racket. In May 1947, he was made head of the local Louisiana crime family and was said to have organized a number of murders, including (if rumors are to be believed) the Kennedy assassination.

At his federal bribery trial 34 years later, Marcello swore that he was nothing more than a humble tomato salesman employed by the Pelican Tomato Company... although he did own a little property which was estimated to be worth $30-$40 million. His eventual conviction kept him in jail for six years but in 1989 he returned home to resume his life as a husband, father and grandfather of 11.

Carlos Marcello died in his sleep in 1993 at the age of 83. Many called it the end of the "Godfather" era.

Gambling in New Orleans

The ties between New Orleans and the sport of gambling go back to at least 1827, when the first casino in America opened in the city. Not only was the first casino located here, but New Orleans is also credited as being the American birthplace for the game of "craps". The game came to Louisiana with both the French and the Spanish but Bernard de Marigny, nicknamed "Johnny Craps" is given the credit for introducing the game to Creole society after learning it in Paris. The name of "craps" probably comes from "crapaud", or frog, a slang term given to the French. From New Orleans, the game was spread upriver by the "Kaintocks". New Orleans was responsible for the American spread of other games as well, including poker and blackjack.

Legal gambling in the city fell out of favor after the Civil War, but in 1868, the legislature chartered a state lottery to a group who agreed to pay $40,000 toward the operation of the Charity Hospital. The lottery operators offered a $600,000 prize, minus the hospital proceeds and a $15,000 slush fund to pay off state legislators to go along with it. When the deal was in danger of failing in 1877, Confederate generals Jubal Early and P.G.T. Beauregard were hired to appear in full dress uniforms to conduct the weekly drawings. The federal government finally shut down the lottery in 1895 and prosecuted all of the officials who were involved.

Up until 1887, gaming establishments operated openly in the French Quarter, but eventually the police began closing them down. Local enthusiasm for gambling never waned however and the stories say that in the 1930's, Senator Huey Long allowed mobster Frank Costello to install slot machines in the city in return for a contribution to the "widows and orphan's fund". Rumor has it that there are still some of these old one-armed bandits floating about town.

In the 1940's, it was said that there were no open gambling establishments in New Orleans proper but that "in Jefferson Parish, the temples of luck seem to outnumber the temples of God". Several of these "temples of luck" were extremely popular and advertised that fact that they were just minutes away from downtown New Orleans.

One such establishment was the Southport Club, which was said to be owned by local boss Carlos Marcello. Another, more famous place was the Beverly Country Club, which in addition to being operated by Carlos Marcello, was also owned by Frank Costello and famed mobster Meyer Lansky. The club opened originally in 1945, the year before Bugsy Siegel started the Flamingo in Las Vegas. It offered strictly illegal gambling but also offered headliners like Danny Thomas, Rudy Vallee and a number of other popular entertainers and celebrities. In the early 1950's, a Senate investigative committee came to New Orleans to look into the festivities being offered at the Beverly. Not long after, it was closed down. The club did re-open again in 1972 as a dinner theater only, but closed again in 1983 when the building burned.

The years following World War II lead to a crackdown on gambling and dozens of establishments were closed. It would not be until 1991 that legal gambling came back to the city with passage of legislation allowing a lottery, riverboat gambling and a single land-based casino. This did not mean that the course of legal gambling would run smoothly though. Harrah's Casino, which is located at the end of Canal Street near the river, was riddled in controversy and bankruptcy for years before finally opening up.

The Axeman's Jazz....
The "Boogeyman" Comes to New Orleans

One of the most mysterious, and still unsolved, frenzies to grip the city of New Orleans came in the early 1900's with the arrival of the enigmatic "Axeman". Who was this strange and terrifying creature? Ghost, ghoul or something worse?

And while the reign of terror presided over by the Axeman was certainly a dark time in the city's history, it would not be the first time, or the last, that a "boogeyman" would come to New Orleans.

For many years, the fear of the "Needle Men" ran rampant throughout portions of New Orleans. No one knows how the stories got started but these strange figures, thought by some to be medical students out looking for bodies to work on, may have hearkened back to the days of Voodoo. In those days, a mere brush on the street could send an intended victim into seizures, comas or even the throes of death. Some believe the tales of men who passed by unsuspecting people on the street, who are then pricked by unseen needles, came from the same general source.

Were the Needle Men merely the creation of folklore, or were they real? Thousands of people around the city certainly believed in them. In 1924, there was a Needle Man scare in the Carrollton section of the city. It was reported that men were sneaking about on the dark streets, hiding behind trees and in vacant lots, waiting to jump out, stick women with needles and then flee the scene. Skeptics believed that the Needle Men were simply the products of too much Prohibition gin, but women in the area swore the attacks were real.

In the 1930's, the Needle Men returned again, this time stabbing young women while they were seated in movie theaters. The stories claimed that many of the young girls were actually knocked unconscious by whatever foul poison the fiends had dipped the needles into. The young women were then carried off into white slavery and the proverbial "fate worse than death". For months in the downtown theaters, women were screaming and fainting as they cried that they had been stuck with a needle. Eventually, the new spate of Needle Men attacks simply faded away.

In addition to the Needle Men, there was also the Gown Man, a figure that struck terror into the hearts of African Americans in New Orleans for many years. The Gown Man was described as being very tall and thin and wearing a black cap and a black gown that reaches all of the way to the ground. Even though the creature would often appear driving a long, black automobile, many of the women who encountered him believed that he was a ghost. Around the Mississippi River neighborhood where he was usually seen, the Gown Man was known to drop from trees and send his luckless victims screaming for their lives.

A similar character who was known in the area back in the 1890's was the "Hugging Molly". This white-robed character would hide in the bushes along darkened streets and when a young woman would come along, he would jump out and scoop her up into a tight embrace. After hugging her for a few moments, he would vanish back into the shadows and leave the girl trembling, yet unharmed.

Despite the fact that the Hugging Molly's intentions seemed harmless, the town was soon completely unnerved about a chance encounter with the monster. To the black residents, the white robe that he wore conjured up not too distant memories of the drapery worn by the Ku Klux Klan. Eventually, the "attacks" stopped and year later, the mystery of the creature was solved upon the death of a kind, mentally retarded man. In his dingy room, his caretakers discovered the white robes that had belonged to Hugging Molly. The sad man had only wanted a hug and had been afraid to ask for one.

Around 1930, the Domino Man began haunting the streets in the Gentilly section of New Orleans. In those days, this was a sparsely populated area of the city and there were many empty lots with stands of trees and heavy underbrush. Children who passed along the wooded paths on their way to school began to be frightened by a strange creature wearing a white robe and hood and who seemed to have the agility of an ape. He would drop out of the trees, and chase little girls with his arms and hands waving wildly. Moments later, he would vanish by leaping into a tree and scurrying away.

Residents of the area began beating the brush and attempting to track down the bizarre creature. Several men claimed to have shot at the Domino Man and were sure that they struck him before he could disappear. Regardless, he always appeared the next day, completely unharmed. Apparently, his only mission was to frighten children. He never really attacked them or followed them very far. He would simply jump out at them and when they screamed and ran away, he would vanish. The mystery of the Domino Man was never solved, although suggestions to his identity ranged from a spirit to that of a monkey that someone had dressed up as a practical joke.

In March 1914, a new fiend appeared in New Orleans. His name was "Jack the Clipper" and he had women all over the city living in fear. In the span of just a few days, Jack had appeared on the scene and made off with locks of women's hair. Over a period of several weeks, he somehow clipped several inches from the ends of dozens of young school girl's hair. This enigma vanished as abruptly as he came, apparently having satisfied whatever strange fetish he was plagued with.

Then, in May 1918 came the greatest "boogeyman" that New Orleans has ever known. His coming would begin a period of terror in the city that would last for the next year and a half. With the coming of darkness, the residents of New Orleans would spend each night listening to every sound, looking at every shadow and would open their newspapers with trembling hands each morning. The Axeman had come to the city.... and no one was safe.

To this day, the identity of the Axeman remains a mystery. Many believe that he was not a "man" at all, but a supernatural creature that was able to appear and disappear at will. There are others who believe that he was merely a demented serial killer who hacked off the heads of his victims while they slept. We will never really know for sure!

On May 23, 1918, an Italian grocer named Joseph Maggio and his wife were butchered while sleeping in their apartment above the Maggio grocery store. Upon investigation, the police discovered that a panel in the rear door had been chiseled out, providing a way in for the killer. The murder weapon, an axe, was found in the apartment, still coated with the Maggio's blood. Nothing in the house had been stolen, including jewelry and money that were nearly in plain sight.

Detectives quickly went to work on the case and while several suspects were arrested and questioned, all were released for lack of evidence against them. The only clue that was discovered was a message that had been written in chalk near the victim's home. It read: "Mrs. Joseph Maggio will sit up tonight. Just write Mrs. Toney"

Investigators began digging into old files, looking for possible cases that matched the Maggio murders, and to their surprise discovered that three murders and a number of attacks against Italian grocers had already taken place in 1911. The murders bore a striking resemblance to the Maggio crime in that an axe had been used in each and access to each home had been gained through a panel in the rear door. These earlier crimes had been thought to be a vendetta of terror organized by the Mafia. The police, and the Italian residents of the French Quarter, braced themselves for the worst.

Almost exactly a month after the Maggio murder came a second crime. Louis Bossumer, a grocer who lived behind his store with his common-law wife, Annie Harriet Lowe, was discovered by neighbors one morning, lying in a pool of blood. He had been badly injured but was not dead. Beside him was Annie, also injured but amazingly, not dead. Both of them had been hacked with an axe. The weapon was also lying next to Bossumer and was also covered with blood. A panel of the kitchen door had been removed, a chisel was lying on the back steps and nothing had been stolen.

After she regained consciousness in Charity Hospital, Annie first claimed her attacker had been young and very dark, but later, she changed her story and stated that Bossumer had attacked her. The police were skeptical however, never being able to ascertain how Bossumer could have attacked Annie and then fractured his own skull with the axe. After he recovered from his injuries, he was released.

Later on that year, in August, a woman named Mrs. Edward Schneider awakened in the night to see a tall, phantom-like form standing over her bed. She screamed just as the axe fell. A few minutes later, her neighbors found her unconscious with her head gashed and bloody and several of her teeth knocked out. She recovered from her injuries.

A few nights later, an Italian grocer named Joseph Romano was also attacked. This attack was just like the others although Romano did not survive. He died a few hours later and was never able to provide any clue as to the identity of the Axeman.

By this time, hysteria was sweeping through the city. Families divided into watches and stood guard over their relatives as they slept. People went about with loaded shotguns and waited for news of the latest "Axeman sightings". On August 11, the killer was seen in the neighborhood of Tulane and Broad, masquerading as a woman, the rumors said. A manhunt was organized but without success. On August 21, a man was seen leaping a back fence but despite a quickly organized search party, the fiend escaped. Were these sightings real or merely fright-fueled imaginations at work?

While most of the so-called sightings can be attributed to panic among local residents, the Axeman did leave tangible evidence behind as well. Also on August 11, a man named Al Durand discovered an axe and a chisel lying outside his rear door in the early morning hours. His back door had been damaged but had apparently proved too thick for the killer to cut through.

In late August, the rear door of Paul Lobella's grocery and residence was chiseled through. No one was home at the time. The same day, another grocer named Joseph Le Bouef reported that an attempt had been made to chisel through his rear door in the night. Awakened by the noise, he had frightened the intruder away. An axe was discovered dropped on his steps. The following day, another axe was found in the yard of A. Recknagle, who was also a grocer. Chisel marks were also found on his back door.

On September 15, a grocer named Paul Durel found that someone had also attempted to cut through his rear door. A case of tomatoes that had been resting against the inside panel had foiled the attack.

Then, as mysteriously as he had come, the Axeman vanished.... at least for awhile.

In the early morning hours of March 10, 1919 the Axeman struck again. It was perhaps his most terrible crime yet. Mrs. Charles Cortimiglia, wife of a grocer in Gretna, just across the river from New Orleans, awakened to find her husband struggling with a large man in dark clothing who was armed with an axe. As her husband fell in a bloody heap to the floor, Mrs. Cortimiglia held her two-year-old daughter in her arms and begged her attacker for mercy, at least for the child. But the axe came down anyway, killing the little girl and fracturing the skull of her mother.

The police were once again stumped and rumblings began to suggest that perhaps the Axeman really wasn't a man at all. Some claimed that he might be a woman, or a midget, enabling him to slip through the small space that he cut in the doors. But others maintained that he was a creature from the world beyond. How else, they questioned, could all of the witnesses describe the killer as being a "large man" when only a small person could have slipped through the chiseled panels in the rear doors? The killer had to have come in through supernatural means as each door was still locked when the attacks were discovered!

Following the Cortimiglia murders, New Orleans was again filled with terror. The police stated that they believed all of the crimes to have been committed by the same man... "a bloodthirsty maniac, filled with a passion for human slaughter".

And perhaps they were right.... On Friday, March 14, 1919, the editor of the New Orleans "Times-Picayune" newspaper received a letter from a man who claimed to be the Axeman. The letter appeared as follows:

Hell, March 13, 1919

Esteemed Mortal:

They have never caught me and they never will. They have never seen me, for I am invisible, even as the ether that surrounds your earth. I am not a human being, but a spirit and a demon from the hottest hell. I am what you Orleanians and your foolish police call the Axeman.

When I see fit, I shall come and claim other victims. I alone know whom they shall be. I shall leave no clue except my bloody axe, besmeared with blood and brains of he whom I have sent below to keep me company. If you wish you may tell the police to be careful not to rile me. Of course, I am a reasonable spirit. I take no offense at the way they have conducted their investigations in the past. In fact, they have been so utterly stupid as to not only amuse me, but His Satanic Majesty, Francis Josef, etc. But tell them to beware. Let them not try to discover what I am, for it were better that they were never born than to incur the wrath of the Axeman. I don't think there is any need of such a warning, for I feel sure the police will always dodge me, as they have in the past. They are wise and know how to keep away from all harm.

Undoubtedly, you Orleanians think of me as a most horrible murderer, which I am, but I could be much worse if I wanted to. If I wished, I could pay a visit to your city every night. At will I could slay thousands of your best citizens, for I am in close relationship with the Angel of Death.

Now, to be exact, at 12:15 (earthly time) on next Tuesday night, I am going to pass over New Orleans. In my infinite mercy, I am going to make a little proposition to you people. Here it is:

I am very fond of jazz music, and I swear by all the devils in the nether regions that every person shall be spared in whose home a jazz band is in full swing at the time I have just mentioned. If everyone has a jazz band going, well, then, so much the better for you people. One thing is certain and that is that some of your people who do not jazz it on Tuesday night (if there be any) will get the axe.

Well, as I am cold and crave the warmth of my native Tartarus, and it is about time I leave your earthly home, I will cease my discourse. Hoping that thou wilt publish this, that it may go well with thee, I have been, am and will be the worst spirit that ever existed either in fact or realm of fancy.

The Axeman

The people of New Orleans did their best to follow the Axeman's instructions to the letter. Restaurants and clubs all over town were jammed with revelers. Friends and neighbors gathered in their homes to "jazz it up" and midnight found the city alive with activity. Banjos, guitars and mandolins strummed into the night while Joseph Davilla, a well-known local composer, created the theme song for the night. He titled his composition "The Mysterious Axeman's Jazz" and in typical New Orleans fashion, it became a huge hit.

When the sun rose the next morning, it was learned that not a single attack had occurred that night. Even though it's doubtful that every home was filled with the sounds of jazz, the Axeman passed the city by, perhaps well satisfied by the celebration that was held in his honor.

All was quiet for some time, until the night of August 3, 1919. In the darkest hours, a young girl named Sarah Laumann was attacked with an axe while she slept in her locked and shuttered home. She received a brain concussion but she recovered. Although the woman did not die, the attack pushed hysteria in the city to new heights. Miss Laumann was not the owner of a grocery store, she was not Italian and her attacker had not entered through a door panel, but a window. In other words, if he could attack Sarah Laumann, then no one was safe!

Was it really the Axeman though, or an imitator? No one knew for sure.

On August 10, a man named Steve Boca stumbled from his home on Elysian Fields Avenue with axe wounds in his skull. Dripping blood, he managed to make it to his friend's home about a half block away. The friend, Frank Genusa, treated the wounds as best he could and then called for help. The police who searched Boca's house found the classic signs of the Axeman, including the chiseled door panel and the bloody axe left lying on the floor.

On September 2, a local druggist named William Carson fired several shots at an intruder who had broken into his home. The intruder left a broken door and an axe behind, but managed to escape without injury.

Then in October, the Axeman appeared for a final slaughter. A grocer named Mike Pepitone was butchered in his bed during the night. His wife and six children, asleep in the next room, were not touched. The usual clues had been left behind but the authorities were no closer to learning his identity than they had been in the beginning.

But then the horror came to an end. This was the last murder attributed to the Axeman. He was never seen or heard from in New Orleans again. No one would ever learn the true identity of the Axeman... or would they?

More than a year after the Axeman's final appearance, a former New Orleans man named Joseph Mumfre was shot to death on the Pacific Coast. He had been killed by a woman named Esther Albano, who was later discovered to be the widow of the Axeman's last victim, Mike Pepitone.

The police began working to try and untangle the mystery that probably linked Mumfre's murder to the Axeman case. Some curious coincidences were revealed during the investigation. Mumfre had once been the leader of a band of blackmailers in New Orleans who had preyed on Italians. He had also been (for a separate matter) sent to prison just after the first axe murders in 1911. In the summer of 1918, he was paroled... at the same time the Axeman appeared again. Immediately after the Pepitone murder, Mumfre had left New Orleans for the coast and strangely, the Axeman had vanished as well. In spite of this, there was no actual evidence to link him to any of the crimes.

Was Joseph Mumfre the Axeman? Or were there actually several killers, all working together to terrorize the Italian community? Or was the maniac actually what he claimed to be all along... "the worst demon that ever existed either in fact or in the realm of fancy"?

Chapter Three
The "Spirit" of New Orleans

The city of New Orleans, wrote authors Lyle Saxon, Edward Dreyer and Robert Tallant, has more ghosts that there are wrought-iron balconies in the Vieux Carre. As they also noted, it is not surprising that a city with the past that New Orleans has would have more than its share of ghosts. In fact, there are so many hauntings here that on one occasion even the Devil himself came to visit, as we'll see in a later chapter.

Stories of ghosts and hauntings fill the annals of the Crescent City to overflowing. What follows is only a sampling of the hundreds of tales that have been whispered over the years!

According to newspaper accounts, there was a haunted house on Fourth Street in 1933 that was rumored to be so haunted that the owners were unable to keep tenants in it. Finally, for fear that it would be burned to the ground or vandalized, it was given to several impoverished black men who were unable to afford the rent. They were simply asked to stay there to make sure the property was not disturbed. Unfortunately, they were unable to fulfill this simple request, as a single night in the building proved that it was inhabited by ghosts!

Unwilling to sleep in the house, they began spending their nights in a small outer building. They reported many strange things about the house itself, like ghostly faces that would appear at the windows, unexplained lights and knocking sounds that came from unseen hands. Worst of all, on nights when the moon was full, the kitchen door would open and reveal eerie, mist-like apparitions crawling about the floor on their hands and knees.

Later, two elderly ladies moved into the front portion of the house. They too reported the ghosts, and in startling detail. They claimed the apparitions looked to be covered in blood and did some pretty vile things in their presence. According to their story, one ghost pulled off his leg and threw it at the tenants and then proceeded to vomit into the women's shoes. Another dug out his liver and tossed it at a lamp, then produced a mass of worms. A third gouged out his own tongue and then clawed out his eyes. They continued to prey on the ladies for days to come, smashing dishes, ripping up clothing, smearing the parlor sofa with filth, ruining food and more. After a week of this, the two women moved out.

Finally, the owner of the house had the floor torn out of the building and replaced it with a new one. He never offered an explanation as to why he did it, but regardless, the haunting stopped. Although it was never verified, the black tenants in the out building stated that a number of old skeletons were found beneath the floor. Once they were decently buried, the ghosts no longer appeared.

There was once a house on Saratoga Street that was haunted by the ghost of an old miser who once lived there. Throughout his life, the old man had worked hard and spent very little, always hoarding his gold pieces and hiding them in his house. Each night, he would sit by an oil lamp and count and caress each gold coin. "My beautiful children," he would call the gold pieces, as he stacked and re-stacked them and then placed them back into a leather pouch.

One night, perhaps fearful that he was going to be robbed, the old man stole into his backyard and he buried the sack of coins in a deep hole. He planned to return and dig them up in a few days, but unfortunately, he died before he could do so.

The stories say that the miser's phantom soon began returning to look for the gold, journeying from his grave in the cemetery across the street. The ghostly figure would appear in the yard, but would wander aimlessly, as though he could no longer remember where he had buried his treasure. The pale apparition would walk about, wringing its hand, mumbling to his "beautiful children" to reveal their hiding place to him. For years, neighbors watched the scene, hoping to be shown where the gold was buried but the ghost never appeared to find it. Many would-be treasure hunters prowled the area and the yard soon became a field of open holes and tossed-aside soil... but the gold was never discovered.

A portion of Cherokee Street was once the scene of a poltergeist outbreak. One night, a rain of stones and bricks began to fall on a number of houses in the 200 block. It only lasted a short time and then ceased, only to occur again the following night. No explanation could be discovered for where the rocks were coming from. As the strange phenomenon continued on night after night, the police were summoned to look into the matter. They searched the entire block but they could find nothing to explain the bizarre events.

After several days of this, neighbors remembered an old man and a little girl who had lived on the block and who had hated each other violently. No one ever knew what had caused the terrible feelings between them but all could remember the loud arguments and the violent screaming matches. Oddly, the two of them had died within the same week and had been buried in nearly adjoining tombs in the cemetery. Some older residents suggested that perhaps their spirits were still continuing their battles in death.

Shortly after, the girl's parents moved her body to another tomb and the falls of bricks and stones ceased immediately.

Years ago, there was also the tale of the "Ghost Who Walked the Sausage Factory" about a brutal murder that had a hideous and supernatural aftermath. The story concerned a man named Hans Muller, a German immigrant who moved to New Orleans and started a sausage factory. Muller had come to America with his wife, but soon grew tired of her, and began having affairs with some of the young women who worked in the factory.

One night, Muller decided to get rid of his wife once and for all and he clubbed her over the head and dumped her body into meat grinder. In moments, there was nothing of her left. Well, almost nothing... because soon, customers began to complain about bits of bone and cloth in their meat.

Days passed and Muller began explaining to everyone that his wife had returned to Germany. Of course, no one had any reason to suspect otherwise. Then one night, while working in the factory alone, he heard a loud thumping sound that came from the boiler vat. He went to look and suddenly, the hideous ghost of his wife lurched toward him from the shadows. She was covered with blood and most of her head had been torn away. As her gory fingers reached for him, he began to scream and ran shrieking out of the building. The noise understandably woke his neighbors but Muller, considerably calmer by this time, told them that he had suffered a bad dream.

The next day, the sausage shop opened as usual, but Muller was nowhere to be seen. A customer came in late in the morning to purchase some sausage and then returned home to cook it for her lunch. She placed the meat into the frying pan and noticed something odd.... there appeared to be something inside of the meat. She quickly realized that it was a gold wedding ring! She called the police but when they went to investigate, they found that Muller was not at home. A quick search found him at the sausage factory, crouched in the corner, screaming, crying and weeping. He told the police officers that he was hiding from his wife, who was going to come out of the sausage grinder and kill him. They took him away and he spent the remaining few days of his life in an insane asylum.

Soon after, another man bought the sausage factory, but the ghost continued to appear. For months, he had a terrible time keeping the workers on and no one would stay in the building after dark. Finally, the ghost stopped appearing and the new owner learned that

Hans Muller had committed suicide at the asylum at about the same time. Apparently, Mrs. Muller's need for revenge had been satisfied.

One of the oddest stories of a ghost in New Orleans involved a French woman who operated a boarding house in the city in 1925. A run of bad luck started for the woman a short time before several of her boarders dropped dead. While this seems as though it would be a terrible thing, the deaths were actually the beginning of the streak of good fortune that followed. Three of the boarders died in all and each of them left a substantial amount of money to the owner of the house. When a fourth boarder became ill, his brother moved him out of the place and declared that the house was cursed. The last man did manage to recover, but by then, the damage was done.

Gossip began to spread that something strange was going on in the house. Even though the doctors found that all of the deaths that had taken placed had been from natural causes, people still whispered. Embarrassed by the scandal, the lady sold her business and moved to a small cottage in the suburbs, where she managed to live quite comfortably on the money that had been left to her by her former boarders.

Many years later, she told a very odd tale to a close friend about what had taken place in the house.

Just before the first boarder had died, the woman had been very desperate for money. She had no idea where she was going to find the funds to put food on the table. Discouraged, she sat down at the kitchen table and looked around sadly. There was literally no food in the house and dinnertime was drawing very near. Suddenly, in the middle of the room, there appeared a man with snow-white hair who looked at her with a smile and asked that she tell him her troubles.

She was frightened but told the man the problems she had. When she finished, he offered simple advice. Why not let the boarders eat raw turnips? Not surprisingly, the lady protested, saying that no one could live on raw turnips. Besides that, she had always maintained a reputation for her fine cooking and what would her guests say if she began to serve only turnips at her table? The man shook his head and he begged her to try it.

Before he vanished, she asked him his name. "Mark Twain," said the spirit and he promptly disappeared.

So the woman went to the market and spent what little money she had on turnips. When she returned home, she sliced them up and filled every dish that she had with pieces of turnips, cut into all shapes and sizes. She watched fearfully as her boarders assembled for dinner, sat down and began dishing up large quantities of the turnips. Each of them ate heartily and they complimented her on the excellent beef, the vegetables and the wonderful dessert. Yes, each one of them had only eaten turnips.

This went on for some time and the woman began to amass a substantial amount of money from what she saved on buying regular food for the boarders to eat. Soon however, the men began to fall ill and they died, unable to exist on turnips alone. The deaths of the three men made news all over the city, but no one ever learned the secret of her spectral fortune until long after she was dead herself.

In 1907, the people of New Orleans learned of another ghostly figure in their midst, that of a phantom who haunted an area of St. Ann Street, near Royal. The spirit attracted a lot of attention and became known as the "Witch of the French Opera". Each night she was said to descend the steps of the opera house, journey to the corner of St. Ann and Royal and then vanish into a certain rooming house. The rather frightening apparition was said to have white, flowing hair, a bony, ashen face and piercing, reddened eyes. Dozens of people reported the ghost, especially the tenants at the rooming house, who often would meet her in the hallway and on the stairs. The owners soon had a hard time keeping boarders at the house.

There was a legend of tragedy and death behind the appearance of the ghost. The stories said that an older woman who lived in the Vieux Carre had once taken a young lover. After discovering that he had been unfaithful with another, she wrote a letter to the police saying that she would return, and then committed suicide. The following night, her ghost was said to have entered the room where her lover and his younger companion slept and she had turned on the gas and suffocated them.

But even revenge could not ease the suffering of this tormented spirit. For the next dozen years, the ghost made the journey from the opera hose to the room where she had killed the young man and his mistress. Then one day in 1919, a new tenant was cleaning the room and discovered half of a yellowed old love letter between the fireplace mantel and the chimney. Without a thought, she tossed the paper into the fire and then was stunned when the apparition of an old woman suddenly appeared! The ghost cried out and reached for the now smoldering letter, but it was too late..... the brittle paper caught fire and disappeared in a whisper of smoke up the chimney. The witch vanished and that was the last time she was ever seen.

Strangely though, on December 4, 1919, the same night as the ghost's final appearance, the French Opera House burned to the ground. The cause of the fire was said to be "of mysterious origins".

Located on St. Peter Street in the French Quarter is an apartment that, according to reports, is seldom occupied. Apparently, many tenants in the past have abandoned the place after encountering the "otherworldly" occupants of the building.

Back in the 1850's, the building was occupied by a dentist named Deschamps, who had an unhealthy interest in the occult. He decided to experiment with what he believed to be his "supernatural powers" and began attempting to hypnotize a young girl for the purpose of using her as a medium to locate buried treasure. When his experiments failed each time, he began to beat and abuse the girl. Finally, after weeks of beatings, she died from an overdose of chloroform. Deschamps was arrested, tried for her murder and hanged.

In the years that followed, the ghost of the dentist and his victim began returning to the scene of the crime and replaying the deadly events of the past. According to the luckless tenants who encountered them, they always appeared together.

Some say that the author Oliver La Farge once lived in this apartment and that he too encountered these ghosts. Whether he did or not, there have certainly been plenty of other people who have. One young man, who was a tenant in the house, was taking a bath one evening when he was surprised by the glowering apparition of Dr. Deschamps. Terrified, he jumped from the tub and ran naked out into the street! A policeman gave chase and managed to stop him with a few yells and an overcoat. The tenant was so terrified that he refused to set foot in the apartment ever again. His friends had to go there to pick up his clothing and belongings.

In more recent years, the place has become a restaurant and employees here still claim to have encounters with the ghost of the dentist and the young woman whose life he took. Pots, pans and plates have mysteriously moved about in the kitchen. Objects have vanished, only to appear again in different places. They also say that they have heard unearthly voices in the building and the sound of someone calling their name. On more than one occasion, they have also had the unnerving sensation of being touched by a hand that is not a human one.

One questionable tale of New Orleans (although a chilling one) involves an old mansion that was visited by a newspaper reporter back in the 1920's. The young man had been sent on a story by his editor, who wanted him to interview an old Spanish lady who was said to be over 100 years old. When the reporter reached the house, he discovered a crumbling edifice that had been built around 1770 and which had now fallen into a state of disrepair.

He was admitted to the house by an ancient mulatto servant, who led him upstairs and into the presence of "the Senorita". This was the old woman that he had been sent to interview, even though he could barely stand to look at her. She was a revolting old hag with skin like parchment and few teeth left in her mouth. However, she was covered with priceless jewelry and even wore a jewel-encrusted tiara on her nearly hairless head.

As the Senorita began to talk, the reporter realized that her sanity had left her long ago. Even though her father had been dead for more than 70 years, she still spoke of him as though he were alive and away on a trip to Spain. She also still believed that she was a young girl and chatted away about her lovers, who were always wealthy Spaniards who came to New Orleans to try to win her hand in marriage. She spoke long of her own beauty and of the wonderful parties that her father would host in her honor when he returned.

The reporter began to find her growing increasingly strange as she continued to speak, hinting that her lovers never left the mansion after they once called upon her. They never wanted to, she told him, as they were so enraptured by her that they would do anything she wanted. One lover, she confided, had even poisoned his own mother so that he could give the

Senorita her jewels. She spoke whimsically of the house's rose garden, saying that she had enjoyed many of her trysts with her lovers there.

During the interview, she constantly gave orders to her servant concerning a great dinner that night, although no dinner was ever prepared. Eventually, the old woman drifted off the sleep and with that, the bizarre interview came to an end.

Leaving the old woman snoring in her chair, the reported slipped off down a corridor and began to explore the decrepit old house. From out of the shadows there suddenly appeared a ghostly man who was clad in dirty and outdated clothing. The apparition was totally silent but managed to convince the nervous reporter to follow him into a room at the end of the hall. When he stepped inside, he was greeted with the sight of scores of other phantoms, all of them young men and all of them long dead.

Terrified, the reporter somehow slipped away from them and crashed down the staircase to the first floor. He ran from the gate and he never returned to the house.

When the Senorita died, about a year later, the new owners of the house began renovating the decaying property. In the process, they tore down the north wall of the rose garden and beneath it, made a horrible discovery. Buried here were the tangled skeletons of as many as 50 young men! Apparently, the Senorita's lovers had never left the rose garden after all!

Chapter Four
The Legend of the
LaLaurie Mansion

The Dark History of New Orleans' Most Haunted House

The haunted history of the LaLaurie Mansion in New Orleans is perhaps one of the best known stories of haunted houses in the city. For generations, it has been considered the most haunted house in the Vieux Carre and in many early writings of the city, it has been referred to simply as "the haunted house". While such a title is more than a little vague, everyone seems to know exactly what house the storyteller is referring to!

The origins of the ghostly tales centering on 1140 Royal Street begin around 1832, when Dr. Louis LaLaurie and his wife, Delphine, moved into the mansion in the French Quarter. The house had not been the first one on this site and for many years, the location was known as the Remairie place. During the colonial history of New Orleans, Jean and Henri Remairie had lived here. Later, another house was built and the property passed into the hands of Barthelmy Lois de Maccarty, the descendant of an Irish gentleman who had acquired a title from the French government. Delphine LaLaurie was the daughter of de Maccarty and had been married two times before she married the doctor.

The house that is now located on the site was built by Delphine's father, but it came into her possession after her marriage to Dr. LaLaurie. The mansion itself was said to be wondrous. According to a "Daily Picayune" newspaper article from March 1892, the house was said to be "grand, even in its decay". The author of the article, Marie L. Puents, wrote: "It towered high above every street in the French Quarter... a large, solid rectangular mass, with its three stories and attic and gray stuccoed front and sides... The walls and ceilings of the deep white portal-way are curiously ornamented by a pair of great gates of open ornamental ironwork... within a marble hallway is a great wide door... and there rises and iron-railed staircase, that winds like a spiral column to the drawing room and sleeping apartments above."

The author also goes on to describe the interior of the house. "The drawing rooms are spacious and the different doors that lead to them, and the great folding doors between, are ornamented with panels beautifully carved in flowers and human faces. All around the walls of these great rooms there extends a frieze covered with railed work representing angels with folded wings and holding palm branches; the lofty ceilings and framework of the doors are

A Historic Photograph of the LaLaurie Mansion

beautifully carved with stars and raised garlands of flowers. The fireplaces are high and old-fashioned.... the chandeliers are rare and quaint... the windows, high and wide, measure seven feet across, and are set between fluted Corinthian pilasters, and open upon a broad balcony....

"At the end of one of these rooms, there was some years ago a little door with large iron hinges.... many strange stories have been connected with this door," the author wrote, "thrilling, bloodcurdling stories!"

Shortly after moving into the mansion, the LaLaurie's became renowned for their social affairs and were respected for their wealth and prominence. Madame LaLaurie became known as the most influential Creole woman in the city, handling the family's business affairs and carrying herself with great style. Her daughters from her previous marriages were among the finest dressed girls in New Orleans, even though one of them was crippled or suffered from some deformity. She was rarely seen at public or social gatherings.

Madame LaLaurie was considered one of the most intelligent and beautiful women in the city. Those who received her attentions at the wonderful gatherings could not stop talking about her. Guests in her home were pampered as their hostess bustled about the house, seeing to their every need. They dined on European china and danced and rested on Oriental fabrics that had been imported at great expense. One of the things that nearly all of her guests recalled about her was her extraordinary kindness.

But this was the side of Madame LaLaurie the friends and admirers were allowed to see. There was another side. Beneath the delicate and refined exterior was a cruel, cold-blooded and possibly insane woman that some only suspected.... but others knew as fact.

The finery of the LaLaurie house was attended to by dozens of slaves. Many guests to her home remembered her sleek, mulatto butler, a handsome man who wore expensive livery and never ventured far from her side. During dinner parties, she always left a sip of wine for him in her glass.

The other slaves that were sometimes seen were not so elegant. In fact, they were surprisingly thin and hollow-chested. It was said they moved around the house like shadows, never raising their eyes. It was concerning these slaves that the rumors about Madame LaLaurie began to circulate. The stories said that she was brutally cruel to them. She kept her cook chained to the fireplace in the kitchen where the sumptuous dinners were prepared and many of the others were treated much worse. In fact, the treatment of them went far beyond cruelty.

It was a neighbor on Royal Street, a M. Montreuil, who first began to suspect something was not quite right in the LaLaurie house. There were whispered conversations about how the LaLaurie slaves seemed to come and go quite often. Parlor maids would be replaced with no explanation or the stable boy would suddenly just disappear... never to be seen again. He made a report to the authorities, but little, if anything, was done about it.

Then, one day another neighbor was climbing her own stairs when she heard a scream and saw Madame LaLaurie chasing a little girl, the Madame's personal servant, across the courtyard with a whip. The neighbor watched the girl being pursued from floor to floor until they at last appeared on the rooftop. The child ran down the steeply pitched roof and then vanished. Moments later, the neighbor heard a horrible thud as the small body struck the flagstones below. The woman also claimed that she later saw the small slave girl buried in a shallow grave beneath the cypress trees in the yard.

A law that prohibited the cruel treatment of slaves in New Orleans caused the authorities to investigate the neighbor's claims. The LaLaurie slaves were impounded and sold at auction. Unfortunately for them, Madame LaLaurie coaxed some relatives into buying them and then selling them back to her in secret. She explained to her friends that the entire incident had been a horrible accident. Some believed her, but many others didn't and the LaLaurie social standing began to slowly decline.

The stories continued about the mistreatment of the LaLaurie slaves and uneasy whispering spread among her former friends. A few party invitations were declined, dinner invitations were ignored and the family was soon politely avoided by other members of the Creole society. Finally, in April of 1834, all of the doubts about Madame LaLaurie were realized.....

A terrible fire broke out in the LaLaurie kitchen. Legend has it that it was set by the cook, who could endure no more of Delphine's tortures. She stated that she would rather be burned alive than endure anymore of her master's abuse. Regardless of how it started, the fire swept through the house. Flames began pouring from a window on the side of the house and smoke filled the rooms. The streets outside began filling with people and soon the volunteer fire department was on hand carrying buckets of water. Bystanders began crowding into the house, trying to offer assistance.

Throughout the chaos, Delphine remained calm. She directed the volunteers who carried out the expensive paintings and smaller pieces of furniture. She was intent on saving the house but would not allow panic to overcome her.

Montreuil, the neighbor who had first aroused suspicion about Madame LaLaurie, came to assist during the fire. He asked if the slaves were in danger from the blaze and was then asked by Delphine not to interfere in her family business. Montreuil then appealed to Judge Canonge, a local official who was also present. They began searching for the rest of the servants and were joined by a man named Fernandez and several of the fire fighters. They made an attempt to reach the upper floor of the house, but found locked doors barring the way. Finally, they discovered a locked wooden door with iron hinges that led to the attic. Dr. LaLaurie refused to open it, so they broke the door down.

What greeted them behind the door is almost beyond human imagination. They found more than a dozen slaves here, chained to the wall in a horrible state. They were both male and female.... some were strapped to makeshift operating tables... some were confined in cages made for dogs.... human body parts were scattered around and human organs were placed haphazardly in buckets.... grisly souvenirs were stacked on shelves and next to them a collection of whips and paddles. The men were forced back, not only from the terrifying sight, but also from the stench of death and decaying flesh in the confined chamber.

According to the newspaper the New Orleans "Bee", and the accounts of those who were present that day, all of the victims were naked and the ones not on tables were chained to the wall. Some of the women had their stomachs sliced open and their insides wrapped about their waists. One woman had her mouth stuffed with animal excrement and then her lips had been sewn shut.

The men were in even more horrible states. Fingernails had been ripped off, eyes poked out, and private parts sliced away. One man hung in shackles with a stick protruding from a hole that had been drilled in the top of his head. It had been used to "stir" his brains. Various wounds and cuts also marred his body and maggots infested the holes. The tortures had been administered so as to not bring a quick death. Mouths had been pinned shut and hands had been sewn to various parts of the body. Some of them were unconscious and some cried in pain, begging to be killed and put out of their misery.

The men fled the scene in disgust and doctors were summoned to provide aid for the tortured slaves. It is uncertain just how many slaves were found in Madame LaLaurie's "torture chamber". Several of them were dead but there were a few who still clung to life.... like a woman whose arms and legs had been removed and another who had been forced into a tiny cage with all of her limbs broken than set again at odd angles. A few of them, and only a few, were strong enough to be able to leave the "chamber of horrors" under their own power.

As the mutilated slaves were carried and led out of the house, the crowd outside gathered around. Only one of two friends remained beside Madame LaLaurie. Even her husband had disappeared. Delphine's mulatto servant acted quickly. He slammed the heavy door that led to the street and quickly locked it. He then hastened to the courtyard and locked the large wooden gates. This effectively sealed the LaLaurie household off from the crowd outside, which was still milling about, waiting to see if any arrests were going to be made. Nothing happened over the course of the several hours that followed.

Needless to say, the horrifying reports from the LaLaurie house were the most hideous things to ever occur in the city and word soon spread about the atrocities. It was believed that Madame LaLaurie alone was responsible for the horror and that her husband turned a blind, but knowing, eye to her activities.

According to the newspapers "at least 2000 people" came to the Cabildo to see the slaves that had been taken from the mansion. Here, they received medical care and those who were conscious were prodded with questions about their captivity and abuse. A long wooden table was filled with instruments of torture that had been brought from the attic. They included whips, shackles, knives and crude medical equipment, some of which was crusted with the red stain of dried blood.

One of the statements taken that day came from a female slave who testified that Madame LaLaurie would sometimes come and inflict torture on the captives while music and parties were going on below. She would come into the attic still clad in her ball gown and lash the slaves as they cowered on the floor. After a few lashes, she would appear to be satisfied and would leave. The mulatto butler would sometimes accompany her. What perverse pleasures she had taken from her "medical experiments" were not spoken of. One of the women also testified that Delphine once beat her own crippled daughter for bringing food to the starving slaves.

Passionate words swept through New Orleans as curious crowds came to gape at the starving and brutalized slaves. As the wounded creatures gulped down the food that was given to them, Judge Canonge, Montreuil, Fernandez and a Felix Lefebvre all made formal statements to the authorities about their discovery of the attic chamber.

In the meantime, the mob was still waiting outside the gates to the house on Royal Street. They expected to see arrests being made and for the authorities to come and demand entrance to the house. Hours passed though and the police did not arrive. The mob continued to grow. More and more people came and as each hour would pass, they would grow more restless and belligerent. Soon, threats were being shouted at the shuttered windows and calls for vengeance were heard from the street.

Suddenly, late in the afternoon, the gates to the high-walled courtyard burst open and a carriage roared out of the gates. It plowed directly into the mob and men scattered before the angry hooves of the horses. The mulatto servant was atop the box and he lashed his whip at the horses and at the faces of those nearby. The coach pushed through the crowd and disappeared from sight, racing down Hospital Street and down toward the Bayou Road.

It all happened so quickly that everyone was taken by surprise. Someone cried out that the carriage had been only a decoy, that Madame LaLaurie was actually escaping through a rear door. While some went to look, others swore that she had been in the carriage, alone. Dr. LaLaurie was nowhere to be found. Her daughters, it was discovered afterward, had been forced to escape the house by climbing over a balcony and into a house next door.

But it was Delphine who the angry mob was after and she had easily escaped their clutches. The carriage drove furiously along the Bayou Road and it is said that a sailing vessel waited for her there and left at once for Mandeville. Another story claimed that she remained in hiding in New Orleans for several days and only left the city when she realized that public opinion was hopelessly against her. No one knows which of these stories is true, but we do know that she was in Mandeville nearly 10 days later because she signed a power of attorney there that would allow an agent in New Orleans to handle her business affairs for her.

The seething mob that remained behind continued to grow. Her flight had enraged the crowd and they decided to take out their anger on the mansion she had left behind. The New Orleans "Courier" newspaper reported that "doors and windows were broken open, the crowd rushed in, and the work of destruction began".

Feather beds were ripped open and thrown out into the street while curtains were dragged down from the window and pictures torn from the walls. Men carried furniture, pianos, tables, sofas and chairs and hurled them out the windows to see them splinter on the streets below. After destroying nearly every belonging left in the house, the mob, still unsatisfied, began to tear apart the house itself. The mahogany railings were torn away from the staircase, glass was broken, doors were torn from their hinges and worse. The mob was "in the very act of pulling down the walls" when the authorities arrived with a group of armed men and restored order. It was later suggested that the house itself be completely torn down, but cooler heads prevailed and instead the house was closed and sealed. It remained that way for several years, silent, uninhabited and abandoned... or was it?

Madame LaLaurie and her family were never seen again. Rumors circulated as to what became of them.... some said they ran away to France and others claimed they lived in the forest along the north shore of Lake Pontchartrain. According to the author George W. Cable, Madame LaLaurie made her way to Mobile and then went on to Paris. He went on to say that her reputation preceded her to France and when she was confronted and recognized in Paris, she spent her days "skulking about in the provinces under assumed names".

However, this story is disputed by travelers from New Orleans who later visited Paris. They positively asserted that they met Delphine in the city and that she had a handsome establishment there. Her gracious manners and style had made her a guest in the most exclusive circles in Paris. They also said that when the stories of what happened in New Orleans reached the French capitol, they were looked upon simply as a result of her well-known "eccentricity" and her uncontrollable temper. This temper, some said, almost bordered on insanity.

But whatever became of the LaLaurie family, there is no record that any legal action was ever taken against her and no mention that she was ever seen in New Orleans, or her fine home, again.

Of course, the same thing cannot be said for her victims.....

The stories of a haunting at 1140 Royal Street began almost as soon as the LaLaurie carriage fled the house. The mansion remained vacant for a few years after its sacking by the mob, falling into a state of ruin and decay. Many people claimed to hear screams of agony coming from the empty house at night and saw the apparitions of slaves walking about on the balconies and in the yards. Some stories even claimed that vagrants who had gone into the house seeking shelter were never heard from again.

The house had been placed on the market by the agent of Madame LaLaurie in 1837 and was purchased by a man who only kept it for three months. He was plagued by strange noises, cries and groans in the night and soon abandoned the place. He tried leasing the rooms for a short time, but the tenants only stayed for a few days at most. Finally, he gave up and the house was abandoned.

Following the Civil War, Reconstruction turned the empty LaLaurie mansion into an integrated high school for "girls of the Lower District" but in 1874, the White League forced the black children to leave the school. A short time later though, a segregationist school board changed things completely and made the school for black children only. This lasted for one year.

In 1882, the mansion once again became a center for New Orleans society when an English teacher turned it into a "conservatory of music and a fashionable dancing school". All went well for some time, as the teacher was well known and attracted students from the finest of the local families.... but then things came to a terrible conclusion. A local newspaper apparently printed an accusation against the teacher, claiming some improprieties with female students, just before a grand social event was to take place at the school. Students and guests shunned the place and the school closed the following day.

A few years later, more strange events plagued the house and it became the center for rumors regarding the death of Jules Vigne, the eccentric member of a wealthy New Orleans family. Vigne lived secretly in the house from the later 1880's until his death in 1892. He was found dead on a tattered cot in the mansion, apparently living in filth, while hidden away in the surrounding rooms was a collection of antiques and treasure. A bag containing several hundred dollars was found near his body and another search found several thousand dollars hidden in his mattress. For some time after, rumors of a lost treasure circulated about the mansion.... but few dared to go in search of it.

The house was abandoned again until the late 1890's. In this time of great immigration to America, many Italians came to live in New Orleans. Landlords quickly bought up old and abandoned buildings to convert into cheap housing for this new wave of renters. The LaLaurie mansion became just such a house but for many of the tenants, even the low rent was not enough to keep them there.

During the time when the mansion was an apartment house, a number of strange events were whispered of. Among them was an encounter between an occupant and a naked black man in chains who attacked him. The black man abruptly vanished. Others claimed to have animals butchered in the house; children were attacked by a phantom with a whip; strange figures appeared wrapped in shrouds; a young mother was terrified to find a woman in elegant evening clothes bending over her sleeping infant; and of course, the ever-present sounds of screams, groans and cries that would reverberate through the house at night. The sounds, they said, came from the locked and abandoned attic.

It was never easy to keep tenants in the house and finally, after word spread of the strange goings-on there, the mansion was deserted once again.

The house would later become a bar and then a furniture store. The saloon, taking advantage of the building's ghastly history was called the "Haunted Saloon". The owner knew many of the building's ghost stories and kept a record of the strange things experienced by patrons.

The furniture store did not fare as well in the former LaLaurie house. The owner first suspected vandals when all of his merchandise was found ruined on several occasions, covered in some sort of dark, stinking liquid. He finally waited one night with a shotgun, hoping the vandals would return. When dawn came, the furniture was all ruined again even though no one, human anyway, had entered the building. The owner closed the place down.

In 1923, the house was renovated and sold to William Warrington, who established the Warrington House, a refuge for poor and homeless men. For the next nine years, the house opened its doors to penniless men who were released from jails and prisons. In 1932, the mansion was sold to the Grand Consistory of Louisiana, an organization like the Freemasons, who kept the place for the next decade. They sold the house in 1942.

In 1969, the mansion was converted into 20 apartments before its current owner, a retired New Orleans doctor, purchased it. He restored the house to its original state with a living area in the front portion and five luxury apartments to the rear. Apparently, tenants are a little easier to keep today than they were one hundred years ago.

Since moving into the place, the owner has reported no supernatural activity and residents who live nearby are unable to recall any recent ghost stories about the mansion. Back in the early 1970's, a tenant named "Mrs. Richards" claimed to witness a number of strange events in her apartment like water faucets turning on by themselves, doors opening and closing and a number of minor annoyances. Other tenants often spoke of the familiar bizarre noises and the lingering story of a young girl's screams that could be heard in the courtyard at night. Since that time, the house has been quiet, leading many to believe the haunting here has simply faded away with time.

Is the LaLaurie house still haunted? It doesn't seem to be, but one has to wonder if the spirits born from this type of tragedy can ever really rest?

A number of years ago, the owners of the house were in the midst of remodeling when they found a hasty graveyard hidden in the back of the house beneath the wooden floor. The skeletal remains had been dumped unceremoniously into the ground. When officials investigated, they found the remains to be of fairly recent origins. They believed that it was Madame LaLaurie's own private graveyard. She had removed sections of the floor in the house and had hastily buried the bodies to avoid being seen and detected. The discovery of the remains answered one question and unfortunately created another. The mystery of why some of the LaLaurie slaves seemed to just simply disappear was solved at last..... but it does make you wonder just how many victims Madame LaLaurie may have claimed?

And how many of them may still be lingering behind in our world?

Chapter Five
The Voodoo Queen of
New Orleans

No book of ghost stories and strange tales of New Orleans would be complete without mention of Marie Laveau, the unchallenged "Queen of Voodoo" in New Orleans. This mystical religion is as big a part of New Orleans as jazz, Cajun food and Mardi Gras. Strangely, many people believe that Voodoo is a thing of the past but they couldn't be more wrong. There are a number of Voodoo shops, and even a museum, operating in the Vieux Carre today. It is as alive, and taken just as seriously, as it was in the days of Marie Laveau.

However, despite the many thousands of people who have been involved in Voodoo, there has been no practitioner of the religion greater than Marie Laveau. Because of this, no look at Voodoo in New Orleans would be complete without a mysterious glimpse of the woman who made it so famous.

And at the ghostly tales which keep her memory alive today.....

Voodoo!

The actual religion of Voodoo, or "Voudon", originated from the ancient practices of Africa. Voodoo came about most likely in Santo Domingo (modern day Haiti) where slaves devoted rituals to the power of nature and the spirits of the dead. The term "voodoo" was probably adapted from the African Fon spirit, "vodu".

For many enslaved Africans, such spiritual traditions provided a means of emotional and spiritual resistance to the hardships of life. In time, slaves from the Caribbean were brought to New Orleans and they brought Voodoo with them.

The first reference to Voodoo in official documents came in 1782 during the Spanish regime in New Orleans. In a document that tells of imports to the colony, there is a terse line regarding black slaves that have been brought from the island of Martinique. Governor Galvez states "these Negroes are too much given to voodooism and make the lives of the citizens unsafe". Galvez was not a man given to superstition and fear. In fact, he was a primarily a soldier and as he made an attempt to ban the importation of slaves from Martinique for a brief time, its likely he felt he had a good reason.

Voodoo had already made its way to New Orleans, but things continued to get worse. In both 1791 and 1804, a series of slave revolts rocked Haiti. The revolts were based around the practice of Voodoo and they ended with the French being expulsed from the island. Many of the French were able to escape to New Orleans and many of them brought their slaves with them. Now, New Orleans had not only additional Voodoo practicing slaves, but rebellious ones as well.

From the very beginning of the New Orleans colony in 1718, the white colonists had been given trouble by the beliefs of their black slaves. Shiploads of slaves came through the city on a regular basis and were bought and sold for manual labor and household work. Hundreds and hundreds were brought to America from Africa, packed into ships and treated like animals.

The earliest shipments of slaves to the colony consisted of captives taken from Africa. In a swamp near New Orleans was a slave farm, said to be a place of horror, where the Africans were kept until they were either "tamed" or killed. Here, they were taught to use field implements, to plow, use an ax, cook and other skills that would be useful to their future owners. Once they were "broken in", they were then brought into the city for auction or sold to individual owners.

These slaves, most of whom spoke no French, had brought with them their religions, beliefs, charms and spells from Africa and Haiti, but soon learned that they were forbidden to practice their own religions by their masters. Many of them were baptized into the Catholic Church and later, the use of these Catholic icons would play a major role in their new religion of Voodoo. These icons would take their place in the Voodoo hierarchy and be worshipped as if they were praying to the God of the Catholic Church.

Many of the Catholic saints would become "stand-ins" for important Voodoo deities and if you go into a Voodoo shop today, you will see statues, candles and icons depicting various Catholic images. There are in fact, Voodoo symbols as well.

Soon after the introduction of the African slaves to New Orleans, Voodoo began to play a major part in the traditions, and fears, of the general populace. It was not long before the white colonists also began to hear of it and to feel its power. By the end of the century, Voodoo was firmly entrenched in the culture of New Orleans.

The religion was practiced by the slaves and the free blacks as well and so strong was the power held by the upper echelons of the religion that they could entice their followers to any crime, and any deed. Whether or not these priests held supernatural power or not, the subtle powers of suggestion and of secret drugs made Voodoo a force to be reckoned with.

Masters felt the taste of poison in their food, women and men the taste of lust with a handful of powder... and even death was held in check by the use of "zombie" drugs. There was no denying that Voodoo was real, and powerful, and even today, it is widely practiced in the south and in the Caribbean islands.... and even in New Orleans.

Marie Laveau

No tales of Voodoo in New Orleans are complete without mention of Marie Laveau, the undisputed Queen of Voodoo. During her lifetime, she was the source of hundreds of tales of terror and wonder in New Orleans. She was born on Santo Domingo in 1794. Her father was white and she was born a free woman. The first record of her in New Orleans was in 1819, when she married Jacques Paris, another free black. He died in 1826 and Marie formed a liaison with Christophe Glapion, with whom she had she bore a daughter, also named Marie, in February 1827. During her long life (she lived until 1881) she gave birth to fifteen children.

That same year, Marie embraced the power of Voodoo and became the queen of the forbidden but widely practiced culture. She was a hairdresser by trade and this allowed her access to many fashionable homes in the city. In this way, she and her daughters had access to an intelligence network that gave Marie her "psychic" powers. She knew everything that was going on in the city just by listening to her customers tell of gossip and scandals.

Marie became a legend in New Orleans, which is particularly amazing in such a segregated culture, but she was more than just a Voodoo practitioner. Marie had an imaginative mind and has been credited with changing Voodoo into much more than just an African superstition. It was Marie who brought the Virgin Mary into Voodoo as the central figure of worship and she borrowed freely to bring Catholic traditions into the culture.

She dealt in spells and charms, for both white and black customers, and produced "gris-gris" bags to cure their ailments. The small bags would be filled with an assortment of magical items and curative roots and could be used to work both good and bad magic. Many have tried to portray Marie as some sort of "evil" sorcerer, but this could not be further from the truth. If anything, she was a clever and astute businesswoman who knew how to use her beliefs, and the beliefs and fears of others, to her own advantage.

One tale of Marie Laveau has reached legendary status in New Orleans. During the height of Marie's power, a young man from a wealthy family was arrested and charged with a series of crimes. While the young man himself was innocent, the true perpetrators had been several of his friends and they had let the blame fall upon their unlucky companion. The grief-stricken father sought out the assistance of Marie and explained the circumstances of the case to her. He promised a handsome reward if she would use her powers to obtain his son's release.

When the day of the trial came about, Marie placed three peppers into her mouth and went into the St. Louis Cathedral to pray. She remained at the altar for some time and then gained entrance to the Cabildo, where the trial was to be held. Before the proceedings could begin, she managed to deposit the three peppers beneath the judge's chair. They were in a spot where they could not be seen by the spectators, but couldn't be missed by the judge when he walked into the courtroom. One can only imagine his feelings over spotting the peppers and then spying the recognizable face of Marie Laveau among the people in the courtroom!

After a lengthy deliberation, the judge returned to the courtroom after hearing all of the unfavorable evidence against the young man and pronounced him to be "not guilty". Was it the supernatural power of Voodoo at work... or did the judge fear what might happen to him if he found the man to be guilty? Remember that Marie possessed the secrets of many of the most influential people in the city. Did the judge have his own secrets to hide?

No matter how she had managed it, the father of the freed youth was ecstatic over the verdict and in return for her help, he gave her the deed to a cottage at 1020 St. Anne Street, between Rampart and Burgundy. It remained her home until her death a number of years later.

Marie died in June of 1881 but many people never realized that she was gone. Her daughter stepped in and took her place and continued her traditions for decades to follow.

Today, Marie and her daughter still reign over the shadowy world of New Orleans Voodoo from the confines of St. Louis Cemetery No. 1. Both are entombed in this cemetery in two-tiered, white stone structure. Or are they?

Marie Laveau's Famous Tomb

The actual site where Marie Laveau's remains are located has been the subject of controversy for many years. Most believe the crypt in St. Louis Cemetery No. 1 holds the bodies of Marie and her daughter, Marie II, but there are many others who do not think so. You see, there is also a "Marie Laveau Tomb" in St. Louis Cemetery No. 2. This is not really a tomb at all, but an "oven" crypt that is within the wall of the cemetery itself. These "ovens" are a typical kind of burial place in New Orleans. They are built into the thick walls of the cemetery and are one on top of another, usually about four high. They can be rented and should the family fail to meet the rent, the remains can be removed and burned.

The "oven" where some people believe Marie II is entombed is located at the rear of the cemetery. The slab is always covered with literally hundreds of red crosses, inscribed with pieces of brick. Is this the true tomb of Marie Laveau? Maybe, and then again, maybe not... some believe this to be the burial place of another Voodoo priestess, Marie Comtesse.

There are also tales that claim Marie is buried somewhere else altogether, including

Girod Street Cemetery, Louisa Street Cemetery and Holt Cemetery.

Some believe the confusion started after the body that was originally buried in the Laveau tomb was later moved. It is said that Marie was first buried in St. Louis Cemetery No. 1 but that her spirit "refused to behave". People became so scared that they refused to go near the cemetery so another priestess, Madame Legendre, and some relatives, moved Marie to Holt Cemetery. She was re-buried in an unmarked grave so that her name would not be remembered. The ghost stayed put from that point on, the story said, but her name has yet to be forgotten.

Regardless, New Orleans tradition holds that Marie is buried in St. Louis Cemetery No. 1 and literally thousands have come here in search of her crypt. The tomb looks like so many others in this cluttered cemetery, until you notice the markings and crosses that have been drawn on the stones. Apart from these marks, you will also see coins, pieces of herb, bottles of rum, beans, bones, bags, flowers, tokens and all manner of things left behind in an offering for the good luck and blessings of the Voodoo Queen. Once, in the 1940's, a sexton of the cemetery told author Robert Tallant that he had found a pair of false teeth that had been left behind here!

But does Marie's spirit really rest in peace? Many believe that Marie returns to life once each year to lead the faithful in worship on St. John's Eve. It is also said that her ghost has been seen in the cemetery and is always recognizable thanks to the "tignon", the seven-knotted handkerchief that she wears.

It is also said that Marie's former home at 1020 St. Ann Street is also haunted. Many claim that they have seen the spirit of Marie, and her ghostly followers, engaged in Voodoo ceremonies there.

There is another house also that may harbor Marie's ghost, located on Chartres Street. It was built in 1807 and according to legend, Marie lived there for a time. Residents of the house claimed that an apparition appeared in the house and hovered near the fireplace. They claimed that it was the ghost of Marie Laveau.

Perhaps the most unusual sighting of Marie's spirit took place in the 1930's when a man claimed to be in a drug store near St. Louis Cemetery No. 1. He was speaking to the druggist when an old woman in a white dress and a blue tignon came and stood next to him. Suddenly, the druggist was no longer listening to him, but looking in terrible fear at the old woman instead. Then, he turned and ran to the back of the store. The man turned and looked at the old woman and she started laughing "like crazy", he said. He thought that perhaps the druggist had been frightened of this "poor crazy woman" who lived in the neighborhood.

Finally, the woman looked at the man and asked if he knew her. He replied that he didn't and she laughed some more. Then, she turned and looked behind the counter. "Where the drugstore man go at", she questioned the young man, now seeming very angry. He shrugged and at that, she slapped him across the face. Moments later, she turned and ran out the door and, to his shock and surprise, vanished over the cemetery wall. Stunned, the man then stated that he "passed out cold".

When he woke up, the druggist was pouring whiskey down his throat. "You know who that was?" he asked the man but the other was still unable to talk. "That was Marie Laveau. She been dead for years and years but every once in awhile people around here see her. Son, you been slapped by the Queen of Voodoos!"

Chapter Six
The Octoroon Mistress

Located at 734 Royal Street in the Vieux Carre is a building that serves as home to one of the city's most enduring ghostly legends. It is that of the "Octoroon Mistress", a beautiful spirit who only appears here on the darkest nights of December. It is a time of year when even the warmth of New Orleans is tempered by cold winds, icy rains and sometimes even freezing temperatures.

They say that she walks on the rooftops of this building, completely naked and unprotected from the cold. She ascends a narrow old staircase that leads from the attic and then steps out onto the roof. As the wind slices around the eaves, this breathtaking phantom huddles in misery with her arms wrapped about her as if they can somehow shield her from the elements. The stories say that she huddles here throughout the night, only to slip away into oblivion as dawn begins to color the sky. Those who have seen her, and have come to search for her in the night, will find no trace of her in the darkness and yet the apparition will return to the rooftop the following evening. She seems doomed to repeat these actions, but only on the coldest nights of the year.

Who was the mournful figure in life? And why does she haunt this chilling rooftop?

According to the legends of the French Quarter, her name was Julie, but it's possible that she was not a slave as some people believe. It is actually more likely that she was the octoroon mistress of a wealthy Creole man who kept her in an apartment on Royal Street. In the early 1800's, it was common for many rich young white men to keep attractive black women as mistresses in the city. These wealthy sons of plantation owners sometimes supported these one-fourth or one-eighth mistresses in addition to their "legitimate" white families. Even though these young women carried only a trace of African blood, marriages and open relationships with them were considered forbidden.

These women were not prostitutes but proper, educated young women. They were all free women and widely known for their beauty. The Creole gentlemen who "kept" these young ladies would support them in fitting style, usually giving them the deed to a small cottage or paying the rent on an apartment in the Vieux Carre. Many of these arrangements would last for years, or perhaps for a lifetime. In addition, many of the ladies became well known for their business establishments, while other simply enjoyed the fineries the arrangements allowed them. They were unhampered with jobs or families and were content to enjoy what being a white man's mistress would allow them in the segregated world of that time period.

This was certainly the case with Julie. Her life was simple and filled with plenty of food, fine clothing, expensive jewelry and more. She was content in such things, until she made the mistake of falling in love with the man who gave her such a lavish lifestyle. Such an emotion would not seem so terrible in a different time and place but because of the fact that black blood ran through her veins... a more permanent arrangement than what she already enjoyed could never take place.

When Julie would explain to her protector that she loved him, he would always reply that he loved her as well. He did everything that he could to try and make her happy. He gave her gifts and new dresses and made sure that she had enough money so that she would never want for anything. The only thing that he was unable to give her though, was to make her his wife.

It was this one thing that Julie wanted more than anything else. She begged and pleaded with him, sometimes angry and sometimes sad, but each time, his answer remained "no". In those days, even a drop of African blood was unacceptable in New Orleans society. The young man's very livelihood depended on the generosity of his family. No matter how much he loved Julie, he could not shame the family by married a black woman.

Julie's anger turned to despair and soon, her lover was not so eager to come to the Royal Street apartment. His fine gifts, and even his love for her, did not seem to be enough and so finally, he agreed to her demands.... but under conditions that he never dreamed that she would try to meet.

"I will marry you, Julie," he told her, "but only if you do one thing to prove your love to me. You must take off all of your clothes and go up onto the roof until morning. I know that it is cold, but if you love me enough, your love will keep you warm. If you will not do this, then our marriage can never be and we will go on in just the way that we are."

The young man must have spoken these words in the belief that Julie would never do such a reckless and stupid thing. It was the middle of December and New Orleans was suffering under a cold spell. Rain and sleet were pelting the windows even as he spoke. He was sure that Julie would laugh at his demands and see the ridiculousness of them being married. Then, he believed, their life could get back to normal.

To his surprise, Julie agreed to do what he asked, although he was sure that she would never go through with it.

During the short time they spent together that evening, darkness fell on the city and the cold rain and monstrous winds battered the house. A fire blazed in the apartment's fireplace though and the young couple remained safe and warm in each other's arms. There would be no more talk of marriage this evening.

Later on in the night, there was a summons at the front door and the young man admitted a friend who had planned to come by and play chess with him. Together, they sat down in the parlor and began drinking and laughing over a chessboard. Soon, all talk of weddings, and perhaps even Julie herself, was briefly forgotten.

But Julie did not forget. As midnight approached, She removed all of her clothing and slowly climbed the steps to the roof. As she reached the outer door, she began to shiver uncontrollably. Icy tendrils of air slipped in around the door frame and danced over her naked flesh. She bit her lip and pushed on, intent on enduring the price that he demanded of her. She pushed open the door and walked out into the cold and frightening blackness.

What happened next we can only imagine. The young gentleman remained with his friend until nearly dawn. Bleary-eyed, he made his way back up the stairs to climb into bed for a few blessed moments of sleep. Curled up next to his beautiful Julie, he knew that time would pass sweetly. He must have pictured her warm and supple body as he opened the door to her bedchamber.

The stories say that he was stunned with horror at what he discovered there. Her bed was empty and her night clothes lay in a heap on the floor. The room itself was silent and deserted. A cry left his lips as he ran for the attic staircase. He never thought she would go through with it! As he made his way out onto the roof, he spied the crumpled body of his lover... cold, frozen and lifeless.

And every December, Julie still walks that lonely rooftop. Her naked body bends to the force of the freezing wind and as dawn approaches, she falls limply to the roof and then vanishes into the ether.

The occupants of the building, which now houses "Bottom of the Cup Tea Room", maintain that strange things do not only occur on the rooftop. For many years, previous tenants claimed that, when the house was quiet and deserted, footsteps would sound in the chamber that once belonged to Julie. They also stated that a young man playing chess would often materialize in the one of the rooms. Perhaps this is Julie's lover, paying an eternal penance for his role in her death?

Today, Julie apparently tries to make her presence known in various parts of the brick townhouse. Staff members at the Tea Room claim to have heard tapping sounds that they cannot identify, along with a ghostly perfume that comes and goes without explanation. They have also seen her spectral reflection in a fish pond in the building's back courtyard and once spotted her apparition rounding a corner.

Many feel that Julie has never left this place. Could the memories of the past be holding her here? Perhaps... for in addition to being the scene of her horrible death, this building is also the scene for her most wonderful memories of life as well.

Chapter Seven
Pere Dagobert
Phantom of the St. Louis
Cathedral

According to the legends of New Orleans, on certain rainy nights, in the hours before dawn, the crisp, clear voice of a man can be heard singing the "Kyrie" in the air around the St. Louis Cathedral.

The St. Louis Cathedral, just beyond Jackson Square.

"Kyrie eleison, kyrie eleison," the eerie voice echoes over the stone streets and off the buildings of the French Quarter. The voice can be heard, they say, coming from everywhere and from nowhere at all. They say this voice is that of a ghost but no accompanying apparition can be seen. It is merely the sound of a man, his rich tones sounding through the dark, wet night.

The story behind this phantom voice is one of the lingering legends of the city and it may be one of the oldest ghost stories that New Orleans can boast.

The owner of the spectral voice was a priest named Pere Dagobert. He arrived in New Orleans in 1745 to pastor the Church of Saint Louis, now the St. Louis Cathedral. He was a very popular and beloved man and he was more than just a priest to the people. He cared for the sick, was the benefactor of the poor and the widowed and was embraced by the people. He was also most decidedly a Frenchman, which may have been what caused the people to love him as they did. He was known as a worldly, but godly man.

He had a voice that was sometimes compared to that of an angel's and parishioners often sighed in dismay on the days when other Capuchin friars would conduct the services. On such days, Pere Dagobert would be most likely off relaxing at the Capuchin plantation on the river. He was known for his discriminating taste in wines and fine foods and for his impeccable manners and good looks.

The people soon grew to love him and it was said that no girl in the colony would have consented to marriage if Pere Dagobert did not perform the ceremony. At the time of death, he must be present to say the final rites. At births, he was the first to be told so that he could perform the impending baptism. If a man needed counsel, Pere Dagobert always knew a way out of trouble. When it came to wedding feasts, gala events and dinner parties, the hosts could always count on the kindly priest to be present. By 1756, he had become the permanent pastor for the church and a permanent fixture in New Orleans.

In October of 1764, the acting governor of Louisiana announced to the colony of New Orleans that the land of the city had been given in treaty to Spain. The people suddenly found themselves citizens of Spain and terror erupted in New Orleans. The French families organized support and petitioned the king of France not to cede New Orleans to Spain but the petition failed. Not long after, the first rebellion began to boil in the New World.

In March of 1766, the first Spanish governor, Don Antonio de Ulloa, arrived in New Orleans. He was instantly hated and a plot began to be hatched to overthrow the Spanish. The ringleaders of the plot were some of the wealthiest and most prominent men in the city and all were friends of Pere Dagobert. In 1768, they organized the first revolutionary expedition of Americans against a European government. The ranks were made up mostly of Acadians, who had been told they were going to be sold into slavery by the Spanish government. The rebellion was successful and by November 1, Don Antonio had escaped to Cuba and the rebels took prisoner his three aides.

But Spain would not give up the colony without a fight.

His Majesty Carlos of Spain and sent a fleet of 24 ships and a 2,600 man mercenary force to New Orleans to re-take the city. It was under the command of Don Alejandro O'Reilly, an Irish expatriate, now fighting for Spain. The commander would soon earn the nickname of "Bloody" O'Reilly, thanks to the events that soon followed his arrival in the city.

O'Reilly quickly learned that mass arrests and intimidation would get him nowhere as he tried to learn the names of the men behind the rebellion. He believed that if he could get to the ringleaders, he could destroy any further resistance. He sent out spies, who mingled with the inhabitants of New Orleans, and who shortly assembled a list of ten suspects.

In October 1769, all ten men were arrested and put on trial. O'Reilly himself as a judge and jury and on October 24, five of the rebel leaders were shot to death by a firing squad. They included Nicholas de Lafreniere, Jean Baptiste Noyan, Pierre Caresse, Pierre Marquis, and

Joseph Milhet. A sixth man, Joseph Villere, was stabbed to death with a bayonet while awaiting trial and also died.

The short-lived revolution was crushed but it is here where the story of rebellion ends... and a more ghostly tale begins.

The men were killed but O'Reilly refused to allow them to be buried. The corpses were left out to rot in the rain and heat. The people were shocked and appalled, not believing that a Catholic would allow these men to not be buried decently. But there was nothing to be done as the bodies were placed under the watchful eye of the Spanish garrison.

But something happened one night that has never been explained....

The mourning families were each visited by Pere Dagobert, who brought food and some small comfort to them. He appeared at their homes and one by one, he brought them to the cathedral and locked them in a small room. As darkness grew deeper, he came and went, each time leaving a sobbing woman and sometimes a few sleepy, frightened children behind. No lights burned in the room and they waited there in the darkness, nibbling at the bread he gave them and sipping at the wine and milk.

Then, at some point in the early morning hours, Pere Dagobert opened the door. He held a lighted candle in his hand and he silently beckoned the families to follow him. They entered the cathedral and there they discovered that the bodies of the six slain ringleaders had somehow appeared there. A dark cloth covered each of the bodies on the floor. How Pere Dagobert had managed to "spirit" these bodies into the church, and from under the noses of the Spanish authorities, is still unknown.

A funeral mass was held and then, in the driving rain, the families managed to get the bodies to the cemetery, where each was entombed. The graves were then sealed in such a way that no traces of the burials could be found.

The miracle was never forgotten by the city's French and Pere Dagobert remained a mysterious and beloved figure in the city until his untimely death in 1776. He was interred in a crypt beneath the altar of the cathedral and many believe that he has never left this place, still content to watch over his parishioners from the other side. They believe that it is Pere Dagobert's voice that has been heard singing the "Kyrie" near the old cathedral and his spirit is still keeping watch over New Orleans more than two centuries after his death.

Chapter Eight
Phantom Army of New Orleans

Hauntings of the Beauregard-Keyes House

During the daylight hours, the Beauregard-Keyes House in the French Quarter plays host to visitors and tourists from across the country, all stopping in to see the rooms with antiques and artifacts of the past. But some say at night, after the tourists and guides have left for the day, other visitors come to this house... spectral travelers from a time long past. The sounds of gunshots and cannon fire fill the air, the sounds of screaming and men and horses howling in agony as the battlefields of the Civil War are recreated inside the walls of this house!

One of the very first reputedly haunted houses I ever visited was the Beauregard House in New Orleans. I remember walking the streets of the French Quarter with my parents and being in awe of the buildings, sights and sounds around me. It was a special day for me. It was my first time in the Crescent City and I was determined not to miss a thing. I badgered my parents into taking me to St. Louis Cemetery No. 1 and past Madame LaLaurie's mansion on Royal Street. I found the cottage where Marie Laveau once lived and finally, just a few blocks from our hotel, I discovered the Beauregard House.

I wish that I could tell you that something unearthly happened that day... but it didn't. Still, I will never forget the feeling that I had walking up the steps and into the building. My first real haunted house!

General Pierre Gustave Toutant Beauregard was one of the leading generals of the Confederate Army. He was the man who gave the order to fire upon Fort Sumter in April of 1861, he was responsible for the stunning southern victory at Bull Run and will always be remembered as for both his successes and his failures...like the terrible defeat at Shiloh. After the war, the general returned to New Orleans and settled into the house at 1113 Chartres Street in the French Quarter.

It is said that this house, with its granite staircases and wrought-iron lacework, was built in 1827 by Joseph Le Carpentier, the grandfather of Paul Charles Morphy, the world's greatest chess player. Morphy was born in this house, in the second room to the left of the hall, in June 1837. It is unknown exactly when General Beauregard moved into the house, but tradition holds that he was Major Beauregard then, still fresh from the Mexican War.

After the Civil War, General Beauregard returned to New Orleans and continued a distinguished, though non-military, career. He took a position as a chief engineer for a railroad, became involved with a streetcar company, became the supervisor for drawings of the Louisiana State Lottery and wrote three books about the Civil War.

There is no record that the house was haunted before the general's death in 1893, or for many years afterward, but it did become the scene of death and tragedy a short time later.

In 1909, the house was purchased by the Giacona family, a well-to-do Italian clan who were known for their dinner parties and gala affairs. One night, neighbors reported hearing the sounds of gunshots and angry shouting at the house. When the police arrived, they found three men dead and a fourth man wounded. The victims were identified as members of the Mafia and it was learned the Giacona's had been victims of an attempted extortion plot. When the family wouldn't pay off, mobsters came after them but the family was ready and killed the would-be assassins.

The attempt to wipe out the family was repeated several times in the years that followed and the Giacona's maintained the house like a fortress. Finally, in the early 1920's, they moved on to more peaceful territory.

In 1925, the new owners of the house decided to convert it into a macaroni factory. A number of concerned residents in the area became worried about the loss of this historic site and an association was formed to buy the house and turn it into a museum to General Beauregard and the Civil War. It later became a National Historic Site.

In the years following World War II, rumors began to surface about the sounds of men in battle coming from the house and from the garden behind it. The sounds were not those of modern arms either.... but the sounds of Civil War period pistols, muskets and cannons.

What was going on at the house? Could the residual energies of the Giacona family have been left behind, leaving an imprint on the atmosphere because of the violence that took place? Or could the Civil War itself have left behind an impression, even though no battles had ever taken place at, or even near, the house? Or stranger still... could the books written by General Beauregard have left an impression behind? Perhaps the general's vivid recollections of bloody battles like Shiloh had, in some strange way actually created their own "ghosts"? Could this be possible?

No one knew for sure and the people who managed the house weren't talking. The staff members denied for years that anything strange was taking place at the house. The director of the house in 1977, Alma H. Neal, denied all of the stories in an interview with author Richard Winer. "We do not know of anything supernatural taking place here," she said. Recent tour guides have stated that the stories are "old wives tales".

But are they really?

While the stories of the "phantom army" are quickly dismissed by contemporary tour guides and by the director of the house, Marion Chamblon, they do admit that odd things do sometimes occur here. "This is a very old house and it can get a little creepy, not scary, at times," she said in an interview with author Frank Spaeth. "If we do have ghosts or spirits here then they are happy ones, and they leave us alone and we leave them alone."

Mrs. Chamblon has always been skeptical of the stories about the ghostly army but can cite other tales from the Civil War era. According to one legend, General Beauregard and his wife once planned a grand ball in the house but unfortunately, the general had to leave the city on business and the party never took place. The story says that every once in awhile the ghosts of General Beauregard and his wife return to the ballroom to host the festivities that never took place.

A fanciful tale of the French Quarter? Perhaps, but it doesn't end there! Some years ago, a young woman rented the apartment that is located below the ballroom. The next morning, when the girl was asked how her night was, she replied that she had been unable to sleep much. She seemed quite disgruntled over the fact that someone in the house had been playing music and moving furniture around all night. Strangely though, no one else had been in the house that night.

One spectral occupant of the house, Chamblon admits, is a cat. "I was standing there one time and the door blew open and my dress moved," she told author Jim Krane, gesturing toward the doors to the dining room porch. "The people here said 'What's that?' I said 'It's just our cat, our little ghost cat. We call it Caroline'".

In addition, the house also boasts a ghostly dog as well. The dog, the caretakers agree, is the spirit of "Lucky", a cocker spaniel that was owned by the house's other famous resident, author Frances Parkinson Keyes. A few days after the novelist died in 1970, Lucky died as well. Friends stated that the animal was pining away with a broken heart for her master. Many believe that Lucky's spirit has remained behind in the house.

Chamblon related a story about a blind woman who visited the historic home with a seeing-eye dog. When they entered the bedroom that belonged to Keyes, the dog stiffened and began to shake with fear.

"Oh, you must have another dog in here," the blind lady said, noticing her own animal's nervousness.

The caretaker replied that the dog must have a very keen sense of smell because there had not been another dog in the house since 1970.

But the other woman shook her head. "No," she replied, "he only acts like this when he actually sees another dog."

Chapter Nine
The New Orleans
Way of Death

The History & Haunts of the City Cemeteries

The cemeteries of New Orleans are much like the city itself. The graveyards are a mirror to the opulence and desecration of a mysterious and enchanting city. They dance back and forth between beauty and ruin. Like New Orleans, the city cemeteries hide secrets... secrets that most will never discover.

The culture of New Orleans is one rich in history and diversity. It is unique among all other cities in America. The city's "way of death" may be the most distinctive part of its culture. For more than 200 years now, the people here have housed their dead in small, above ground tombs. They are built along streets in miniature cities of the deceased and the forgotten. These cities of the dead provide hours of discovery for the intrepid seeker and for the brave of heart. For not only ghosts lurk here, but the thief and the brigand as well.

To understand the strangeness of the New Orleans cemetery culture. We must return to the beginnings of the city itself. You see, for the entire length of its existence, New Orleans is a city that has known death. Just a few short years after the colony was founded, it was flattened by a hurricane, bringing ruin and destruction. For years after, the impoverished colonists saw their numbers reduced by the grim reaper.

The city was always wet then, as it continues to be today. The original site of New Orleans, which is the French Quarter today, had a water table just beneath the soil. The land sloped back from the river toward Lake Pontchartrain, falling quickly below the level of the sea. The question soon arose.... where would the colonists bury the dead in such water-logged conditions?

The highest area in the region was along the banks of the Mississippi. The natural levees there had been created by years of soil being deposited by the river's current. This was the first site chosen for burial of the deceased. During floods (which came often) though, the bodies of the dead would wash out of their muddy graves and come floating through the streets of town. Obviously, this was considered a problem.

There were other burials as well, although not much is known about where exactly they took place during this period. Internments during the colonial days were beneath the ground and no markers remain. Old documents have revealed that during an auction of lots along Rampart Streets, remains of the dead were removed from that area and transferred to a square that is now surrounded by Bienville, Chartres, Conti and Royal Streets. In 1743, this burial ground was again moved to a site that was opposite the Charity Hospital of that day, in a square bounded by Toulouse, St. Peter, Burgundy and Rampart Streets. In 1788, it was transferred once more beyond the ramparts of the old city and one block south.

When Basin Street was cut through, the cemetery, now outside of the original city, lost all of the ground between Basin and Rampart Streets. Bones that were dug up in that immediate vicinity as late as 1900 seem to support the theory held by many historians that St. Louis Cemetery No. 1 is actually only a portion of the cemetery that was started in 1788. There may be many other bodies that are forever lost in time.

Around 1725, a new graveyard was created outside of the city. The priests of the St. Louis Church oversaw it. It could only be reached by a winding path from town. This was not done for aesthetic reasons, but for ones of health. It was commonly believed that graveyards exuded a noxious odor that carried disease. Combined with the marshy soil of the area, it was considered to be an unhealthy place. For this reason, the cemetery was placed outside of town as a precaution against infection in a town already known for its high death rate.

The cemetery was known as St. Peter Street Cemetery. Most of the burials here were below ground and space was reserved for the clergy and the wealthy and distinguished of the city. In spite of this, the cemetery, which has long been built over, was said to be as shabby and dirty as New Orleans itself in those days. The cemetery remained a prime burial spot for many years, until finally, it was simply filled to capacity.

During the years of 1787 and 1788, New Orleans saw much in the way of death and hardship. The city was rocked with plague and disease, claiming many lives. Malaria, smallpox and influenza took their toll on the city and hundreds died. St Peter Street Cemetery became so overcrowded that reports claim the bones of the dead commonly protruded from the ground. There was simply no other place to put the newly departed.

The following year, a fire broke out on Good Friday and swept through the city, destroying homes, buildings and the parish church of St. Louis. A few months later, a hurricane wiped out another huge portion of the city. Hundreds more lives were taken.

St. Louis Cemetery No. 1

A new graveyard was desperately needed and the St. Peter Street Cemetery closed down for good. The land was sold off for building lots. The first of the now classic St. Louis cemeteries was officially opened in 1789. The new cemetery was a walled enclosure with its main entrance off Rampart Street. The poor were buried here in unmarked graves until the middle 1800's and as available space filled, the level of the soil began to sink. Contracts for dirt were frequently bid upon and city chain gangs shoveled it evenly throughout the graveyard, making room for more bodies. It is believed that beneath the grounds of the cemetery, there are layers of bones several feet thick.

Is it any wonder these labyrinths of the dead breed tales of ghosts?

For all but the indigent though, above ground tombs were the rule. The reasons were obvious as the wet ground of Louisiana caused the graves to fill with water. The coffins would often float to the surface, despite gravediggers placing heavy stones or bricks on the lids. Such conditions made funerals a somewhat terrifying affair. Caskets were often lowered into gurgling pools of water and oozing mud. As often as not, the coffin would capsize as the water began to leak in, causing newly buried and half-decomposed cadavers to float to the surface of the grave... to the horror of those attending the funeral, of course.

A writer for the New Orleans "Courier" newspaper described his own cemetery encounters in June 1833. "The horrid image of this place is still in my mind. I cannot drive it from my imagination," he wrote. "The tombs are all above ground, and those who can afford it will never be buried underground... the graveyard is all on a dead level and on rainy days inundated with water. It is a morass, a swamp party rescued from the wilderness. I followed the procession to the grave. The coffin was taken from the hearse.

"I now watched the process of internment... The body was that of a colored person who had died of cholera.... The grave is not over two feet and a half deep, I measured it for curiosity. The bottom was soft mud into which could be thrust a stick to almost any depth. The water was within a foot of the top of the grave..... The coffin was put into the grave and it floated so as to be level with the surface."

The majority of the burials were soon placed in tombs, however most of the early tombs were not fancy or decorative. Most were simple but functional enclosures and most of the doors were bricked over once the burial had taken place. Years later, architects would design more elaborate tombs for the city's elite, but few of those can be seen in the older graveyards.

Family and private tombs, of which many can be seen in St. Louis Cemetery No. 1, are owned and used by specific families. Individual families have purchased these lots and they have constructed tombs to suit their purposes on the land. Most of them have two vaults and the top vault is used first. As family members die out, the remains are continually moved downward until the tomb is full. After one year and one day has passed since the death of an individual in the vault, the remains can then be moved again and transferred into the "caveau", a chamber in the tomb's foundation. This chamber can house many branches of the family tree and under the Louisiana law of "forced heirship", parents are legally bound to leave their estates to their children. These estates always include the family tombs. The private tombs can be sold however, and they tend to fetch a very high price on the open market.

St. Louis Cemetery No. 1

Another common type of tomb is the wall or "oven" vault. These vaults also serve as the wall of the cemetery. In order to entomb someone in a wall vault, the marble plaque must be removed and then the layer of brick and plaster behind the plaque must be broken open. After that, any casket that is already inside must be removed and disposed of. In the past, these caskets were burned for fear of contagion but today, they are merely thrown away.

Any human remains found in the old casket are then placed back in the vault and moved to the rear or side to make room for the new coffin. The piles of remains in these vaults may be the mingled bones of a number of generations.

The wall vaults are also referred to as "oven vaults", thanks to the fact that the barrel-shaped crypts look like brick baker's ovens. Ironically though, the vaults do act literally as ovens too. In cooler climates, one year and one day would not be enough time for a corpse to decompose. However, in southern Louisiana, the temperature inside of one of these brick wall vaults can reach several hundred degrees between the months of May and September. Such temperatures are a great aid in accelerating decomposition.

Many of these wall vaults are not actually owned, although some are. In most cases, families with less money rent the vaults for burial. As with a home or an apartment, if the rents are not paid on the vaults, the occupants are then evicted.

For those who could not afford a private tomb, but dreaded the idea of the soggy earth, they had the option of the wall vault or a society tomb. The society vaults were the precursor of today's public mausoleums, although most were organized by ethnic origins or associations such as the Orleans Battalion, who were veterans of the Battle of New Orleans.

There are a number of famous residents of New Orleans who are buried in St. Louis Cemetery No. 1 and it has also gained notoriety in other ways as well. Perhaps the graveyard's greatest notoriety came in 1969 with the release of the film "Easy Rider" starring Peter Fonda and Dennis Hopper. In one regrettable scene, the two bikers come to St. Louis Cemetery No. 1, where they proceed to drop acid and then begin a hallucinogenic rampage through the cemetery. The graveyard trek includes nudity, rape and a scene where Peter Fonda climbs onto the lap of the large "Italia" statue on the Italian Society Tomb and begins weeping, having mistaken the statue for his mother.

While the scene is difficult to comprehend, the images from the cemetery were very recognizable, especially to the families in New Orleans who had loved ones interred in the graveyard. Many were shocked that such a scene was filmed on property belonging to the church. As it turns out though, the film crew did not have a permit to film inside of the cemetery and because of complaints from tomb owners, "Easy Rider" became the last motion picture to be shot inside of St. Louis Cemetery No. 1. Since that time, no filming has been allowed in the cemetery with the exception of approved documentaries and educational films.

One famous resident of the cemetery is Homer Plessy, who died in 1925. Plessy was the black plaintiff in the landmark Supreme Court case, "Plessy vs. Ferguson", which established the precedent of "Separate but Equal" for black citizens. The decision was not overturned until "Brown vs. the Board of Education" many years later.

Also interred in the cemetery is Bernard de Marigny, an aristocratic Creole gentleman who family owned much of what is now New Orleans. He died in 1871 but left a permanent mark on the city as the "Marigny" section, on the downriver side of the French Quarter, was once his family plantation.

Another notable is Etienne Bore', a historic New Orleans political figure who was buried here in 1820. He was the city's first mayor, appointed in 1801 after France had re-acquired Louisiana from Spain. He is best remembered today as the first person to successfully granulate Louisiana sugar on a commercial scale. Thanks to this, sugar went on to become one of the state's major cash crops.

Also here is Paul Morphy, America's undisputed chess champion, who died in 1884 and Ernest "Dutch" Morial, who passed away in 1989. Morial was New Orleans' first black mayor, the city's first black judge, the first elected to the Louisiana House of Representatives, the first black to graduate from the LSU law school and even founded New Orleans' first black-owned bank. His son, Marc Morial, followed in his father's mayoral footsteps.

The cemetery's "Protestant Section" also holds the remains of a number of the city's well-known former residents. The Protestant section in itself is interesting in that this is the only part of the graveyard that is separated. In every other section, one can find rich and poor, black and white, entombed side by side. Only by religion are the gravesites segregated. The Protestant section came about after the Louisiana Purchase, which brought the greatest influx of Americans to New Orleans.

This section is noticeably different from the Catholic tombs in the rest of the cemetery. The newly arrived Protestant Americans were not prone to above-ground burials so they interred the bodies of the dead beneath the ground, even though the section is obviously below sea level. Because of this, you can see the double layers of brick and large slabs that have been designed to hold the water-logged coffins below the surface. Legend has it that in the 1800's, visitors to this section of the cemetery often reported the sounds of the coffins knocking and thumping against the tops of the tombs. Ghostly sounds? No, but disconcerting nonetheless.

Two of the most notable citizens with graves in this section are William C.C. Claiborne, the first American governor of Louisiana, and Benjamin Henry Latrobe, the famous architect who died during a Yellow Fever epidemic in 1820. Latrobe had originally been buried in the Girod Street Cemetery, which was deconsecrated and demolished in 1957. Many of the Protestants buried there were moved to this section of St. Louis Cemetery No. 1 and other burial grounds. Somehow though, Latrobe's body was lost in the transfer and what became of him is anyone's guess. Today, only a plaque remains to honor this architectural visionary.

Cemetery Strangeness

Perhaps the most famous person buried anywhere in the cemetery is Marie Laveau. Despite long-running controversies as to whether or not Marie is really buried here, the tomb is the most frequently visited site in the graveyard. It has been generally accepted as her burial place and generations of curiosity-seekers and Voodoo devotees have visited the crypt. Many of them have left offerings behind that include anything from coins, to pieces of herb, beans, bones, bags, flowers, tokens and just about anything else. All of them are hoping for good luck and the blessings of the Voodoo Queen.

In addition to the offerings, you will also finds thousands of markings and X's covering the tomb. The origins of this alleged Voodoo practice are unclear, but despite what some people tell you, it is not an old tradition. A huge number of the X's that you see on the tomb have been left by tour groups and uneducated guides who instruct the members of the groups to leave three X's inscribed on the tomb. This, along with other elements of the ritual, are supposed to get your wishes granted.

Before you do this, you should know that the Glapion family (who owns the tomb) does not consider this Voodoo, but vandalism. If you are hoping to get on the good side of Marie Laveau, leave an offering instead. That way, you're sure not to get anyone mad at you.

If Marie is truly buried in this tomb, does she rest here in peace? Some would say that she does not, based on the legends that say that Marie's ghost sometimes walks the narrow paths of the graveyard. In fact, one man even claimed to have been slapped by her spirit after making a disparaging remark at her tomb one day.

Another tale of the cemetery, and Marie Laveau, springs from the 1930's. According to the story, a drifter with no money or prospects decided to sleep in the cemetery one night. He scaled a tomb and slept fitfully for several hours before being awakened by a strange sound. Thinking that perhaps vandals or grave robbers would injure him, he decided to make his escape to the streets. As he rounded the corner of a row of crypts, he saw a terrible sight. Positioned in front of Marie Laveau's tomb was a glowing, nude woman with her body entwined by a serpent. Surrounding her were the ghostly forms of men and women, dancing in mad but silent abandon. Needless to say, the drifter fled for his life.

Another account of the cemetery is the New Orleans version of the story the "Nail in the Tomb". This legend has crossed the country in many variations, but local folklorists swear that it had its start in New Orleans.. and at St. Louis Cemetery No. 1.

The tale goes that three young men spent a night drinking and carousing in the French Quarter. Their talk soon turned to death, voodoo and Marie Laveau. Before long, one of the men was enticed into a wager. His friends bet him $30 that he would not climb the cemetery wall and drive a spike into the wall of Marie's resting place. He accepted the wager and a short time later, entered the cemetery.

His friends waited for him to return but soon, minutes turned into hours. Dawn came and with it, the opening of the cemetery gates. The worried young men hurried to the tomb and there, they found their friend... lying dead on the ground!

In his drunken state, he had hammered the spike through his coat and into the stone wall of the crypt. As he started to leave, what he believed was an unseen force (actually the misguided nail) held him in place. Panic and fear overwhelmed him and he literally died of fright. But was it really just confusion which fueled his horror, or did he see something on that dark night which so terrified him that his heart couldn't stand it? Those who allege that the cemetery is haunted are certain that it is the latter.

The stories also say that in the 1930's, New Orleans taxi cabs avoided St. Louis Cemetery No. 1 whenever possible.... or at least they never stopped to pick up a young woman in white who hailed them from the graveyard's entrance!

One driver had picked up just such a young girl one night and drove her to the address that she gave him. Once they arrived, she asked him to go up and ring the bell, then inquire for the man who lived there. The man came out, but when the driver told him of the girl waiting in the cab, he immediately asked for her description. When the driver described the girl to him, the man shook his head sadly. This was obviously not the first time that a driver had appeared on his doorstep. The young girl, he explained to the taxi driver, was his wife... but she had died many years ago and had been interred wearing her bridal gown at St. Louis Cemetery No. 1. That was when the driver suddenly realized the white gown the woman was wearing had been a wedding dress!

He raced back to the cab and jerked open the door but the woman was gone. The driver fainted away on the spot. After that, young women in white stood little chance of hailing a cab near the entrance to the graveyard.

By 1820, the city was outgrowing its boundaries, reaching Rampart Street, and the old cemetery became overcrowded. They chose another site, not too far away for the funeral processions, and called it St. Louis Cemetery No. 2. Burials began here in 1823.

The new cemetery was laid out in a perfect square with large, house-like mausoleums on orderly streets. It was the embodiment of the term, city of the dead. Over time, the tombs here became much larger and grander than in St. Louis Cemetery No. 1, although below ground burials continued as well. Contracts for cemetery dirt were constantly filled.

As the city grew, more cemeteries were added but only one other (that I know of) boasts a ghost story. It is called Metairie Cemetery and has always been known as the most fashionable in the city. It became the epitome of the classic Victorian graveyard, which was far removed from the jumbled chaos of St. Louis Cemetery No. 1. Originally a racetrack, the grounds were converted to their present use in 1873 by Charles T. Howard, president of both the New Orleans Racing Association and the Louisiana State Lottery. The circle of the racecourse became the main drive of the cemetery and other roads were laid out, ponds were dug and flowers and trees were planted. Metairie remains an opulent park-like cemetery and holds the grave and tombs of the wealthiest people in the city.

The Moriarty Monument, a stunning shaft that holds four life-sized female figures, marks the entrance to the cemetery. It is said that Daniel Moriarty ordered a sculptor to do a group of "Four Graces" for his wife's monument. When he was informed that there were only Three Graces, Hope, Faith and Charity, he simply shrugged and insisted the monument hold four Graces anyway.

Elsewhere in the cemetery, a statue of Stonewall Jackson watches over a monument to the Army of Virginia. Albert Sidney Johnston rides a bronze horse atop the mound that covers the heroic dead of the Army of Tennessee, which includes the remains of General Beauregard. In other locations are notables like General Richard Taylor, General Fred N. Ogden and General John Bell Hood. At one time, Jefferson Davis was also buried here, but his body was removed.

The most interesting tomb in Metairie does not belong to any Confederate leader or wealthy politician. However, it does belong to "royalty".... to Josie Arlington, the once reigning Queen of Storyville.

Josie Arlington & The Flaming Tomb

For years, the tomb of Josie Deubler, also known as Josie Arlington, has attracted more people to Metairie than any other monument in the cemetery. In fact, curious crowds have sometimes forced police officers to remain all night on the spot to maintain order.

During the heyday of the Storyville district, Josie was the most colorful and infamous madam of New Orleans. In this center of vice is where Josie operated her house of ill repute and became very rich. The house was known as the finest bordello in the district, stocked with beautiful women, fine liquor, wonderful food and exotic drugs.

The women were all dressed in expensive French lingerie and entertained the cream of New Orleans society. Many of the men who came to Josie's were politicians, judges, lawyers, bankers, doctors and even city officials. She had the friendship of some of the most influential men in the city, but was denied the one thing she really wanted... social acceptance.

She was shunned by the families of the city and even publicly ignored by the men she knew so well. Her money and charm meant nothing to the society circles of New Orleans. But what Josie could not have in life, she would have in death. She got her revenge on the society snobs by electing to be buried in the most fashionable cemetery in New Orleans, Metairie Cemetery.

The Maiden Knocks at Josie Arlington's Tomb

She purchased a plot on a small hill and had erected a red marble tomb, topped by two blazing pillars. On the steps of the tomb was placed a bronze statue that ascended the staircase with a bouquet of roses in the crook of her arm. The tomb was an amazing piece of funerary art, designed by an eminent architect named Albert Weiblen, and cost Josie a small fortune. Although from the scandal it created, it was well worth it in her eyes.

Tongues wagged all over the city and people, mostly women, complained that Josie should not be allowed to be buried in Metairie. There was nothing they could do to stop her though and nothing was ever said to Josie's face. The construction of the tomb had achieved just what she had wanted it to do... it had gotten the people's attention!

No sooner had the tomb been finished in 1911, than a strange story began making the rounds. Some curiosity-seekers had gone out to see the tomb and upon their arrival one evening, were greeted with a sight that sent them running. The tomb seemed to burst into flames before their very eyes! The smooth red marble shimmered with fire, and the tendrils of flame appeared to snake over the surface like shiny phantoms. The word quickly spread and people came in droves to witness the bizarre sight. The cemetery was overrun with people every evening, which shocked the cemetery caretakers and the families of those buried on the grounds. Scandal followed Josie even to her death.

Josie passed away in 1914 and was interred in the "flaming tomb", as it was often referred to. Soon, an alarming number of sightseers began to report another weird event, in addition to the glowing tomb. Many swore they had actually seen the statue on the front steps move. Even two of the cemetery gravediggers, a Mr. Todkins and a Mr. Anthony, swore they had witnessed the statue leaving her post and moving around the tombs. They claimed to follow her one night, only to see her suddenly disappear. There were also two occasions when the statue may have traveled about the graveyard! According to records, she was found both times in other parts of the cemetery. Most blamed vandals, but the legends say otherwise.

There were also stories told by people who lived in the vicinity of the cemetery. They claimed that the statue of the "Maiden" would sometimes become angry and begin pounding on the door of the crypt. This spectral pounding would create a din that could be heard for blocks. Anyone who asked about the noises would be told that it was the Maiden "trying to get in." The story was that Josie had lived by a certain rule regarding her bordello in Storyville. The rule was that no virgins would ever be allowed to enter her establishment. The stories say that she placed the statue of the Maiden on the steps of the tomb to symbolize this lifelong code of honor.

Others say that the statue is Josie herself. As a young girl, she stayed out too late, the stories say, and her father locked her out of the house. Even though she pounded on the door and pleaded with him, he would never allow her to enter again. After that, she went away and began a career that made her one of the richest women in New Orleans. Still other agree that the statue may be Josie Arlington, but they say it symbolizes Josie as an outsider to the society circles that she always wanted to be inside of. They say that no matter hard she "knocked", the doors would never open for her.

The tradition of the flaming tomb has been kept alive for many years, although most claim the phenomena was created by a nearby streetlight that would sway in the wind. Regardless, no one has ever been able to provide an explanation for the eyewitness accounts of the "living" statue.

Perhaps Josie was never accepted in life... but she is certainly still on the minds of many in New Orleans long after her death!

Chapter Ten
Madame Mineurecanal
The Creole Lady of
Royal Street

Located just beyond the French Quarter, in the Marigny District, is another house that has been the scene of ghostly apparitions and terror. It is a two-and-a-half story structure right off Franklin on Royal Street and while it may not be as famous as the LaLaurie Mansion or the Beauregard home, it has certainly been just as haunted.

The story really begins in the early 1900's, when the house was owned by a great Creole lady that legends tell us was named Madame Mineurecanal. She was not a famous person, or even a well-known one and in fact, her identity would probably be forgotten today if she had not taken her own life in the Royal Street house.

One night, for reasons unknown, she climbed the narrow staircase that leads to the third floor of the house and here, she fashioned a noose from an old piece of rope that she found. She stood on a chair and reached up to a beam that connected to the attic ceiling. With trembling hands, she tied the rope to the rafter and then stepped back to gaze at her work.

As she stood there, lost in whatever thoughts might be filling her mind, she heard the sound of whimpering at her feet. She looked down and saw her faithful dog, cowering in fear by her side. His small white body trembled, as if he had some idea of what his master planned to do. She suddenly realized that she could not leave the animal to fend for himself after her death, so without a second thought, she lifted him into her arms. She held him for a moment and then she placed her hands about his throat and began to squeeze. The dog struggled for a few moments and then went limp. Now, she hoped, her beloved pet could accompany her to the other side.

She carefully placed the dog onto the floor and then climbed once more onto the wooden chair. The noose was fitted about her neck and then she violently kicked the chair out from beneath her. As her body swung outward from the force of the movement, the chair crashed over backward and clattered onto the attic floor.

Within a few minutes, she was dead. Her last breath was squeezed from her lungs as she died in great agony. She stepped over the line from this world to the next, but in those last tragic moments, did her spirit really leave the house? Those who have encountered her say that it did not!

The house was rumored to be haunted for many years after Madame Mineurecanal's death. Apparently, it was hard to keep tenants in the place, or so the legends said. Despite the spooky tales though, the first real documentation of a haunting came shortly after World War II when the house was sold (cheap... because it was haunted) to a family named Ruez. Because of a housing shortage after the war, there were several families living in the house, including Mr. and Mr. Ruez, their son and his wife, their grandchildren, Ramon and Teresa, and Ramon's two uncles and their families.

In the late 1970's, authors Richard Winer and Nancy Osborn were able to meet with Ramon and Teresa while visiting New Orleans. From these two eyewitnesses, they were able to learn much about the early history of the haunting in the house.

The first person to see the ghost was Mrs. Ruez. She used to sleep in a bedroom on the second balcony landing. One night, she was in her room reading and heard one of the aunt's babies crying. The infant had been put to bed in a crib, a short distance down the hallway. A few minutes passed and the baby continued to cry, so she got up and came to the end of the stairway. She saw a lady with dark hair bending over the crib. The older woman thought that it was the baby's mother and couldn't understand why she didn't pick up the child. She called out to her but the woman ignored her. Finally, after repeating her call again, she stomped her foot and shouted "Rita!", the woman's name. At that, the baby's mother got out of her bed in the other room and came to the doorway where Mrs. Ruez stood. In seconds, the mysterious woman by the crib turned and vanished into the wall near the closet.

The second sighting of the ghost was by Ramon and Teresa's mother. She was in the house alone one day, pregnant with her second child, and went up the second floor to call her husband and see what time he would be coming home from work. At that time, the only telephone in the house was located by the second floor stairway that led up to the attic. While she was dialing the number, she heard what sounded like the patter of a little dog's feet coming down the steps from the attic. She looked up and saw a little white terrier on the stairs. He was followed closely by a dark-haired woman in a long white dress.

"As the woman came closer," Ramon said, "it was obvious to my mother that the form was not human."

She was so frightened that she dropped the phone. She took hold of a religious medal that she wore around her neck and began praying, then ran down the stairs, too frightened to look back. She was in her seventh month of pregnancy at the time she saw the Lady and a few days afterward, she gave birth to the baby and it was stillborn. Ramon and Teresa always believed that the sighting of the ghost and the death of the baby were connected.

After this terrible incident, everyone in the family began to report strange sounds coming from the attic. Sometimes, after midnight, they would hear moaning and the sound of a woman crying in the darkness.

On one occasion, one of the uncles, Santos, was coming home from work late one night and he saw the ghostly lady coming down the staircase from the attic. She walked out to the end of the balcony and then disappeared. On another night, as he was climbing the stairs to his bedroom, he actually had to move aside to let the woman pass him on the steps. He claimed that he could feel an icy-cold wave coming from her. He was so scared that he ran to his bedroom and locked the door to protect his wife and children.

Ramon always remembered that when he and his sister would get into trouble, they would be punished by being forced to sit alone on a couch in the second floor hallway. Nearby was the staircase that led up the third floor attic. He recalled that often when they sat there, they would always see a woman they didn't know walking down the stairs. He described her as being very Creole looking and wearing a white dress. He also said that a little white dog always accompanied her.

Teresa probably saw the woman more than anyone else and started calling her "Mini Canal". She had no idea where the name came from, although her mother asked her repeatedly. She was only four or five years old at the time and no one would have any idea until much later about the tragic history of the house. The story of the suicide would come from an elderly neighbor who had lived on the block for years. She remembered the incident from when she herself was a small child.

Soon, everyone began calling the ghost "Mini Canal", including their cousin, Alfrien, who made the mistake of making fun of the spirit. He walked around the house one day singing "Mini-Canal" over and over again and thoroughly enjoying himself. Later that night, after going to bed, the boy began screaming in his room. When the lights were turned on, his cheek was found to be bright red... as though someone had slapped him!

The hauntings continued to the point that everyone in the house saw, or was affected by the ghost. One night, Ramon's father was lying in bed and he looked up and saw someone he thought was his wife, mostly because of her long, dark hair. He was about to say something to her when he felt something moving in the bed behind him. "He turned around and saw that it was my mother, sleeping," Ramon recalled. "When he looked back at the sofa, there was no one there."

Eventually, the sightings and encounters with the ghost moved past the point of being merely unnerving. "There have been a number of unpleasant things associated with the ghost," Teresa said. "My Uncle Louis saw her and died right afterward in a car accident. He was quite young".

Other tragedies seemed to be connected to the Lady as well. Robert, another uncle of Ramon and Teresa, began to develop emotional problems after his first encounter with the ghost. He would become very shaken and troubled whenever she was seen. One day, he even tried to commit suicide by cutting open his wrists. On another occasion, he was stopped from jumping over the second floor balcony to the landing below. "He didn't seem to remember why he was trying to take his life," Teresa added, "just that he had become terribly depressed without reason."

Teresa also remembered a day when she found her youngest brother hanging by one hand on the outside of the balcony railing. He was only a baby at the time and no one could figure out how he could have possibly gotten there. Another time, when he was only eight months old, he was discovered nearly strangled under strange circumstances. Apparently, he had fallen from his high chair and was hanging from it by his neck. As he was freed, Teresa suddenly began screaming that Mini Canal had tried to hurt the baby. Her grandmother was so angry over the repeated incidents in the house that she picked up the high chair and broke it into pieces.

Eventually, the Ruez family members began moving out of the house. Even though Grandmother Ruez had gotten the house blessed, the strange incidents continued to occur and Madame Mineurecanal seemed intent on remaining behind. Teresa recalled that her family moved out after her mother simply became too frightened to stay there.

The house of Madame Minieurecanal still stands today at 2606 Royal Street. A few years ago, a young attorney from Santa Fe named Phil Hantel heard about the place and moved in. The pink stucco house was a little run down at the time and he assumed that this is why the asking price was so reasonable. He wouldn't hear about the strange goings-on until after he moved in.

Not long after getting settled, he began to hear of an old woman that once lived in the house. The Creole lady had strangled her dog and then committed suicide in the attic, he was told, and her ghost has never left the place. Hantel insists the story is wrong though... the ghost no longer haunts the house!

Madame Minieurecanal was banished long before he moved in. The previous owner of the house had been an American Indian and rituals were allegedly performed in the house to ward off the spirits of the dead. "They burned juniper branches and other stuff to dispel any evil spirits," he said. "I've also heard that she's trapped in the chimney. They performed a service and then capped the chimney."

So, is this house still haunted? According to Phil Hantel it isn't, but one has to wonder what might happen if that chimney was ever opened up. "My neighbor across the street told me not to uncap the chimney," he explained.

Perhaps the Creole Lady is still around after all.....

Chapter Eleven
Le Petit Theatre
du Vieux Carre

Theaters have always been a perfect haven for earthbound spirits. They are dark, often deserted, full of nooks, crannies, empty hallways and strange shadows and they make the ideal place for all sorts of hauntings. Theaters all over the country boast more than their share of ghosts, from the intelligent spirit to the residual energies of the past. The energy, emotions and constant stream of personalities are the vital ingredients for ghostly activity... and this is marvelously apparent at the French Quarter's Le Petit Theatre. Although many theaters can brag about a ghost or two, this particular theater is home to many!

Le Petit Theatre du Vieux Carre opened as a playhouse in the early 1920's and has been operating ever since, presenting plays and musicals to the New Orleans community. Prior to opening as a theater, the building served as a number of other businesses and probably dates back to around 1795. Little information remains as to what may have taken place here in the early years that might cause the location to be haunted. All that we have left today are the legends of the theater itself, and of course, of its ghosts.

Theater ghosts are usually those of people who have a connection to the building. Most stories tell of former actors, directors or stagehands who may have died tragically in the place. There are also tales of staff members who simply became so attached to the theater in life that they refused to leave it in death. Such may be the case of the spirits who still inhabit Le Petit Theatre.

The most famous ghost, by far, is that of "Caroline", a former actress who worked at the theater in the 1920's. There are a couple of different versions of how Caroline met her end in the theater, but both of them conclude with her staying behind to haunt the place. In one story, she was an actress who was having an affair with a director at the theater. One day, as they were trysting on the third story balcony, Caroline accidentally fell over the railing and fell to the flagstone courtyard below. She died there, according to Bill Walker, the theater's technical director, dressed for the evening's performance in a white wedding gown. Her ghost has been at the theater ever since.

The other story claims that Caroline was actually married while she performed at the theater and became involved with another actor, who was also married. The two of them carried on an affair for some time and usually met in a small storage room on the theater's upper floor. No one knows what really happened next, the stories say, but it is believed that Caroline may have committed suicide after her husband discovered that she was unfaithful. She chose to take her life in the one place where she had known her greatest happiness, Le Petit Theatre. She plunged to her death from the window of the third floor storage room and, as in the previous version of the story, plummeted to the stones below.

Regardless of what really happened, Caroline has been said to have never left the premises. Over the years, she has been encountered by dozens of reliable witnesses and has not only been sighted, but has interacted with many of them as well. It seems that she has been instrumental over the years in helping staff members to retrieve lost items around the building. Unlike most ghosts, who are well known for causing items to vanish, Caroline will actually cause things to appear in places where they can be found.

The attic of the theater is a terrible place to be looking for anything. The large room is a jumble of props, costumes and discarded items from past performances. Many staff members have simply thrown up their hands and have given up, rather than search through the mountains of paraphernalia. Others have a simpler, although supernatural, solution. "You'll be looking for something in the attic and can't find it," Bill Walker explains. "So you call out... 'Hey Caroline, where is it?' Then you come back in 15 minutes and it'll be sitting right in the middle of the aisle."

Stephen Thurber, a former assistant technical director at the theater, always maintained that it was a tradition for actors and staff members to ask Caroline for help. He had plenty of his own strange experiences to know that "something" was around to assist them in finding missing props and other items. On one occasion, he searched everywhere for several swords that were needed for a production. He scoured the building and asked everyone if they had seen them, but the swords were simply nowhere to be found. Finally, after several minutes, he was "drawn" to a room that he had already searched. He didn't know why he went back there, but he did. As soon as he opened the door, he saw the missing swords, lying out in plain sight. There was no way that he could have missed them, he was sure, they had not been in the spot the last time that he was in the room.

But not all of the ghosts here are so benevolent. Thurber himself has an encounter several years ago that he would describe as "frightening" to say the least. He explained that he and two colleagues were searching the building for yet another missing prop. When he approached a particular room, he inexplicably became filled with feelings of foreboding and fear. In fact, he became so afraid that he actually told his friends about it. Only after they laughed and told him that he was being irrational was he brave enough to open the door. He gripped the knob in his hand, turned it and started to pull the door open, still fighting the terror that was welling up inside of him. Suddenly, the door to the room burst open and a hazy, human-like figure rushed out of the darkness inside. The figure almost immediately vanished, but not before knocking Thurber backwards and sprawling onto the floor. The contact with whatever the shape had been was so violent that blood was pouring from the assistant director's mouth and nose. His friends could do nothing more than help him to his feet and stare in amazement.

Who was this bizarre and chilling figure? Perhaps it was the anonymous spirit that haunts the place, which was described by author Victor C. Klein. This unnamed actress was said to have also been involved in an affair with a theater director who, despite their involvement, cast another young woman in the lead role of a production. Angry and bitter, the actress chose to take her own life in a fittingly dramatic fashion. Shortly after the curtain opened on the new play, she jumped from the overhead catwalk with a rope tied around her neck. Needless to say, she did not survive the fall!

As the years have passed, it has been said that her miserable spirit provides the feelings of terror and sorrow that have been felt without explanation in the theater. She is also said to be the cold spot that has been experienced on the stage and in other spots in the building. Who this spirit is remain unknown, but there is little doubt that her pain and suffering has caused her to stay behind in this place.

And still, these ghosts do not walk here alone. Another resident spirit is that of a man that staff members simply refer to as "the Captain". The stories say that he was once a regular audience member who fell in love with one of the theater's actresses. He faithfully attended every one of her performances, but passed away before he could express his feelings for her. To this day, he still attends every performance at the theater and has a regular spot where his apparition is often observed... a balcony seat that is located three rows back on the right-hand aisle.

Yet another restless spirit is that of "Sigmund", a former stage carpenter at the theater. He was employed here for many years and in death has returned to play pranks and create mischief on the stage and in the audience. Bill Walker claims that he has been seen by a number of staff members and patrons in the building. "People have supposedly been on stage and looked into the wings and saw him there, he explained. He went on to add that Sigmund has also been blamed for an incident involving the stage curtain. During a performance, it somehow got snagged on a nail that was located 20 feet up on a wall. There was no comfortable explanation as to how this could have happened.

Besides the theater's staff members, who seem to readily accept the spectral occupants of the building, these lonely ghosts have other company as well... a group of ghost children who have been heard laughing and signing in the theater. They have also been known, according to Bill Walker, to pester the office manager. "She was in the front office one day and everything that could be turned on, turned on... the copier, fax machine, the phones, the lights,' he recalled. "She yelled 'Cut it out!' and it stopped."

If the building does indeed have ghostly children about... at least they are well behaved!

Chapter Twelve
New Orleans' Ghosts of the Sea

Ghost stories and ghastly legends have always been a part of the lore of the sea. On some occasions though, the tales of the sea manage to extend themselves to become a part of the "land lubber's" lore as well. Such is the case with two very different stories that each have a connection to New Orleans.

Seaman's Bethel

Many years ago, the Seamen's Bethel on St. Thomas Street was said to be haunted by two ghosts. The property had been purchased by the Presbyterians in 1860 and adapted into accommodations for sailors. Prior to that, a portion of it had been a private residence and it is believed that the stories of the haunting came from this region of the structure.

Not long after the building had been refurbished and renovated, stories began to be told among the residents of strange sounds and apparitions. They spoke of the coming and going of phantom footsteps and two vague forms that would climb the stairs in the night. The ghostly figures would open and close doors and enter into the bedchambers, then leave again. Some remarked that it was almost as if they were searching for someone or something they could not find.

A number of the men swore to being awakened in the night, drenched in a cold sweat, to find these hazy apparitions standing over them. They all claimed to smell rotting fish and sea salt during each such encounter.

This went on for some time and as the sailors departed, new men came in to take their place. The encounters continued and the stories grew. The figures paced up and down the corridors and some added that they heard a faint singing voice that seemed to come from far away and yet always accompanied the appearance of the Bethel's resident ghosts.

Then one night, one of the seamen experienced his fill of the strange events. He saw the wispy shapes enter his bedchamber and rather than cower in fear, he addressed the spirits boldly and demanded to know what it was they wanted. He was overpowered by the smell of fish and the brine of the sea, but then a plaintive voice answered in reply to his question.

"Mother! Mother!", the voice is said to have cried. "Where's Mother? I have brought Julian back to her. Mother, where are you? I never can find you!"

Then, as the sailor told his companions the next day, he raised himself up from his bed and saw the two spirits very clearly for the first time. One of the apparitions appeared as a young seaman in wet and dripping oilskins and by his side stood a little boy with seaweed hanging from his body. They remained there for a moment and then vanished.

The following morning, the sailor told his friends of his adventures the night before. Nearly all of them had encountered the ghosts themselves and had little reason to doubt the strange story. He went on to brag about his bravery in the face of the supernatural, never realizing that he would soon pay a high price for his valor. Two nights later, the sailor died in his sleep. The doctors say that he choked to death on his own tongue, but the other men were not so sure. They stated that his eyes, in death, seemed to be staring at something terrifying that the others could not see.

What had occurred in his darkened room that night? And who were the ghosts that had been encountered in the house for so long?

One seaman, intrigued by the mystery, took it upon himself to discover what had taken place in the Bethel years before. He learned that a family named Weaver had built the house around 1840. Over the course of the next 10 years, they had five children. The youngest of them, the sailor was shocked to learn, had been named Julian. When the boy was very young, perhaps around four of five, he disappeared without a trace. The family, fearing that he had been stolen away by some stranger, searched the country, but they never found him. In spite of this, his mother always clung to the hope that someday he might come back.

Later in life, the oldest Weaver son, Edward, went to sea. His ship was later wrecked and went down in a storm. All of the crew and passengers on board were lost, including Edward. Only one man survived and he later came to New Orleans, where he told the story of the fatal accident. He also told of how Edward Weaver had discovered that his long-lost brother Julian was actually aboard the same ship with him, serving as a cabin boy! The two of them had been joyously reunited and planned at length for their return home.

Unfortunately though, they never lived to return to New Orleans. Only after the sea had claimed them were they able to make it back. The ghosts began appearing in the Weaver house not long after the tragic shipwreck and it was said that certain members of the family actually recognized them. Their mother however, bitter over the fact that fate had stolen her sons from her, refused to believe and forbid her daughters from discussing the idea that the boys had returned from their watery grave.

This did nothing to deter the ghosts from trying to reach out to her though. They often roamed the house and stood over her bed at night, waiting for a welcoming word that did not come. Often, it was said, they would appear outside of her window in the darkness or stand near the front door. The specters were often seen by passing neighbors, who would then run away and lock themselves into their own homes.

The Weaver sisters could do nothing to help the spirits, as it was their mother's affections the ghosts were seeking. Eventually, the neighborhood was so bothered by their presence that the Weaver family moved away. For years afterward, the boys continued to haunt the house, unaware of, or confused about, the changes that had come to the structure.

It is unknown whether or not these unhappy ghosts ever found peace or not. Regardless, after they were questioned by the sailor (who may have paid for the answer with his life), the ghosts of the two boys were never reported again.

The Ghosts of the S. S. Watertown

The New Orleans Cities Service Tanker Dock was once the home port of an oil tanker called the S.S. "Watertown". While the sea boasts many unsolved mysteries, there may not be another as bizarre or as well evidenced as the haunting connected to this ship.

In December 1924, a tragic accident occurred aboard the tanker. Two seamen, James Courtney and Michael Meehan, were cleaning a cargo tank while the ship was on its way to the Panama Canal from the Pacific coast. Both men were overcome by fumes in the hold and died from asphyxiation. In maritime fashion, they were both buried at sea on December 4, 1924.

The following day, the "phantom faces" of the two men first appeared. That same afternoon, the ship's captain, Keith Tracy, received a report from his first mate that two faces were following the ship in the water. Because Meehan and Courtney were popular and had many friends on board, Captain Tracy first assumed the sighting was borne out of grief and depression over the men's deaths. Soon, however, he was also at the rail with the rest of the crew, staring at what appeared to be two men in the water, keeping pace with the ship. They were within 40 feet of the figures when Monroe Atkins, the ship's chief engineer cried, "It's Courtney and Meehan!". The tanker slowed near the two men but they vanished.

All of the crew, including Tracy, agreed that the apparitions were of the two dead men and they witnessed the faces appearing daily as the ship made its way from the Panama Canal to New Orleans. As the ship changed direction, so did the figures, and they kept pace with the vessel as the voyage progressed.

When the ship docked, the Captain reported the bizarre events to officials at the Cities Service Company, who were naturally skeptical. However, J.S. Patton, a supervisor, suggested that Tracy try and photograph the faces on their next voyage. Tracy's first mate owned a camera and volunteered to try and obtain proof of the strange apparitions. Apparently impressed with the testimony of the men on board the ship, Patton gave a sealed roll of film to the Captain, who then officiated as the camera was loaded.

Almost as soon as the "Watertown" left the docks, the phantom faces reappeared. Six photographs were taken of them but the film was re-sealed and not developed until the ship returned to New Orleans. It was then delivered personally to J.S. Patton, who sent it to a commercial developer. Five of the photographs showed nothing, but the sixth revealed the clear images of two ghostly faces. Those who knew the men in life quickly identified them as Courtney and Meehan, the two seamen who had lost their lives in the ship's cargo tank.

Ten years later, a highly inaccurate account of the story behind the faces appeared in the Cities Service Company's own magazine, "Service". It attracted the attention of a paranormal investigator named Hereward Carrington and he began delving into the facts of the case. He attempted to interview those who were involved first hand in the incident, but both Patton and first mate of the "Watertown" had died. The ship's captain and most of the original crew had since dispersed or retired and could not be located. Carrington was able to interview the manager of the company's New York office though, a man named Storey.

The Phantom Figures of the S.S. Watertown

He was able to confirm that the office had once displayed a blow-up of the snapshot that had featured the ghostly faces in it. The photographer who had developed the film could not be traced and even more disappointing, no official report had ever been placed on file in New Orleans.

Carrington was able to glean other facts from the manager though. He learned that the strange figures only appeared on occasion, coming and going and lasting only for a few seconds each time. Strangely, they also seemed to appear in the exact same location around the ship each time. They were also always the same size, a little larger than life-size, and always stayed the same distance from one another. Unfortunately though, he was never able to get a look at the original photograph.

In 1957, another investigator, Michael Mann, also became intrigued by the story. He spent more than five years tracing the facts behind the case and was eventually able to secure a copy of the photo. He also learned that after the photos were taken and sworn to by Captain Tracy and his assistant engineer, Monroe Atkins, the film was checked for fakery by the Burns

Detective Agency. The negatives were returned to Tracy and became the property of the owners of the ship.

As the case was never solved or debunked, authors like D. Scott Rogo maintained an interest in it over the decades. He posed a number of interesting questions... if the figures were so clear that the entire crew saw them, then why did only one of the six photographs testify to their existence? He guessed that perhaps the faces were "real" enough to be collectively seen, but not always clear to be photographed. However, he also realized that whatever force created the images was not strong enough to support their appearance for more than a few moments at a time.

Ultimately, the case remains an unsolved mystery of the supernatural. The phantom seamen eventually faded away and were never seen again. Their disappearance marked the end of one of the greatest and most baffling stories of the sea.

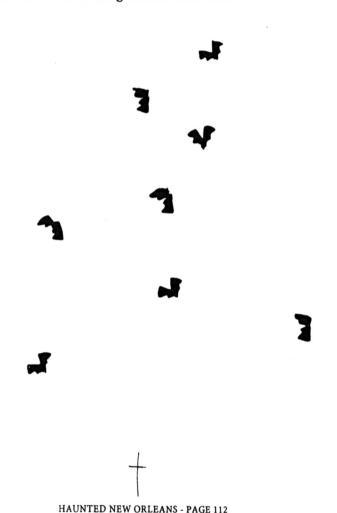

Chapter Thirteen
The Devil Came to New Orleans

The Macabre History of the Fabled Devil's Mansion

New Orleans, they say, is a city that is so haunted and so steeped in corruption that the Devil once came here to live. He resided with his lover for a time in an ornate mansion at 1319 St. Charles Avenue. The legends say that he kept a woman there, an exotic creature with white skin and dark hair, and that he dressed her in the finest silks and presented her with priceless jewels.

Those who passed the house, long after the Devil took his leave of the place, would pointedly walk on the other side of the street. They would point out an image though, which had been left behind on the front gable. It was a mysterious place, steeped in murder, death and sin, and one that passersby and neighbors avoided at all costs!

The Devil's Mansion was a tall, imposing structure that was built sometime in the late 1820's, although no one seems to know the precise date. There are only vague records of the site being acquired and then the house seems to have appeared on the site almost overnight. The strange tales go on to say that the Devil started the house with one room and then added another room to it each night. Apparently, he did a poor job of the construction though, for later legends recall that no two rooms had the same floor level. All over the house, steps led up and down to enter one room after another.

The mansion was built as a home for the Devil's mistress, a stunning French woman named Madeline Frenau. She was said to be a beautiful young woman who wanted for nothing. No servants stayed in the house, the old timers recalled, but the spirits of the dead kept the place clean and served Madeline her meals.

Then one day, the beautiful French woman disappeared without a trace and the house was abandoned. For several years, it remained empty. The windows grew dark and the ornate decor of the mansion was covered with dirt and grime. Vines and mold grew over the bricks and the house began to fall into a state of decay.

Around 1840, the house was sold and a family moved into it. Soon however, they began to speak of ghosts and a terrifying event that was repeated in the house night after night. The family attempted to entertain and hold lavish parties in the mansion, but the place was so forbidding and oppressive that they eventually fled the house in horror.

The spectral events that finally drove them away were centered in the great dining room of the house. The huge room ran the entire width of the mansion and was a shadowed, gloomy place with steps that entered the central hall, the butler's pantry and rear yard. It was here that the bloodcurdling tableau was enacted each night.

No matter what other furniture was present in the room, an enormous dining table would appear in the chamber as the sun began to fall. It would materialize beneath the crystal chandelier and would be covered with white linen. Two places were set at the table with heavy silver, crystal plates and glistening goblets. Before each place setting, a figure would appear.... one of a man and the other a woman with dark hair and alabaster skin. No sound could be heard coming from these phantom diners, although they appeared to be in deep conservation.

Then suddenly, the eyes of the woman would flare and she would rise abruptly from her seat. She would snatch up a cloth napkin into her hands and then pounce upon her companion. The cloth would be twisted around his neck as she pulled it tighter and tighter. His face would turn a crimson color and then blood would burst from his mouth and throat, spewing out over the table. The woman would pull at the knot of the napkin until the man finally ceased to struggle.

The body of the man would then collapse onto the table and the woman would stare at him with some amount of satisfaction. Then, her eyes would turn to her hands, which were stained with the man's blood. Her eyes would then widen in horror and she would attempt to wipe the gore onto the man's clothing, the napkin, the tablecloth and even the curtains of the room. No matter what she touched though, recalled the occupants of the house, she would leave red streaks behind. Finally, she would run from the room, stumbling up and down the many steps, until she would vanish without a trace.

This terrible scene replayed itself over and over again, year after year. Each new tenant that moved into the house, soon abandoned it again. Some stayed a week, others a month and a few only a single night. One act of the macabre play was more than enough to convince them that they wanted no part of the mansion.

Only one family remained in the house for any length of time. This was when Charles B. Larendon and his wife, Laura Beauregard Larendon, the daughter of Confederate General Pierre Gustave Toutant Beauregard, moved into the place. Apparently, the Larendon family witnessed the ghostly murder take place a number of times but somehow they became accepting of it. They loved the house and found that the haunting was a small price to pay for the long halls, comfortable window seats, Italian fountain and the richly carved marble fireplaces.

They remained in the mansion for several years before tragedy struck. Sadly, the infant daughter of Charles and Laura died and then Laura passed away a short time later. Broken and shattered, Charles stayed on in the house and became a virtual recluse. He turned away his family, his old friends and his well-meaning neighbors, and immersed himself in his own sad and lonely world. He had only the ghosts to keep him company and he kept detailed and eccentric journals and diaries of his many experiences with them. His notes eventually unveiled the secrets of the mysterious house and the gruesome murder.

When the Devil built a mansion for his lover, he never dreamed that she would take up his wicked ways and betray him. Madeline had not been ensconced in the house for long before she began to grow lonely and tired of the mansion's lifeless rooms. She was left alone to wander the place while the Devil plied his trade for days at a time. In time, she found her own lover, a young Creole man named Alcide Cancienne. He was a vain and heartless man, but the two of them found such physical pleasure in one another that they were unable to stay apart. He came to the mansion as often as he could, unaware that he had a rival for Madeline's affections.

One night when he came to the house, Alcide was in a foul mood. Madeline asked him what was wrong and he told her of a strange encounter that had taken place a few hours earlier. He had been on his way to her home when he was stopped on the street by a tall, dark-haired man with burning eyes. The stranger pointedly asked him if he knew Madeline Frenau. Alcide replied truthfully that she was his lover and in fact, he was on his way to see her that very moment.

The sinister stranger laughed, showing off a row of sharp-looking teeth, and confessed that he too was Madeline's lover. However, the stranger said, he had grown tired of her. He offered his mistress to Alcide, along with a million pounds in gold, but with one condition.... Alcide and Madeline could leave New Orleans but the two of them had to change their names to "Monsieur and Madame L".

Alcide was puzzled as he told of the experience to Madeline. "What could the 'L' stand for?" he asked her.

She shook her head. "I don't know," she replied, but a cold chill swept through her. She knew that the single initial stood for "Lucifer".

The stranger had told Alcide that he could take Madeline away with him that very night. When she heard this, Madeline was thrilled. She had grown tired of her lonely existence and now dreaded the time she was forced to spend with the Devil and his depraved lusts. She begged her lover to free her from her prison.

To her surprise, Alcide laughed coldly. He too had grown tired of Madeline. There were many other younger and more beautiful women that he could have, he told her. Madeline was the mistress of two men and in his opinion, little better than a prostitute.

Madeline was furious and before Alcide could act, she took a cloth from the table and wrapped it about his neck. With almost inhuman strength, she snapped it tightly about his neck... so tight that an artery burst in his throat and showered Madeline with blood. He slipped forward and collapsed onto the table, a dark stain pooling outward from his body.

For the rest of the night, Madeline tried to wash the blood from her clothing and her body. It would not be washed away though and she left streaks and stains in her wake as she ran about the mansion in a panic. She collapsed onto the floor in the hallway and was soon startled by a dark shadow that crossed the lamp light. The Devil had come home!

He laughed when he saw her and her murdered lover and he lifted Alcide's corpse up onto this shoulder. He entwined the fingers of his other hand into Madeline's hair and he savagely pulled her through the house. They climbed the stairs to the topmost level of the mansion and the Devil shoved her out onto the roof. There, perched on the peak of the gable, he devoured the body of Alcide, leaving only a few shreds of bone and bloody clothing behind. He tossed these down to the alley below and the neighborhood cats fought over the remaining pieces of skin.

But the Devil's hunger was not yet satisfied and he reached for Madeline. Not surprisingly, she began to scream.

The house was abandoned once again after the death of Charles Larendon. A Mrs. Jacques and her family later came to live in the mansion, but they too fled the house in terror. They reported that not only did the scene in the dining room continue to appear, but that the smell of smoke was often present in the house when no fires were lit. In addition, they claimed that doors opened and closed by themselves, locked and unlocked, and that phantom footsteps roamed up and down the shadowy corridors.

It was said that the door to the bathroom seemed to be the focal point of the activity. The knob to this door would turn back and forth, both day and night, as if someone wanted desperately to get in. There was no explanation for this oddity... other than that the ghost of Madeline was still looking for a place where she could wash the blood from her hands!

The house became an enigma to the neighborhood and a place of mystery and rumor. It was finally torn down in 1930 but remained a curiosity until that day. For those who did not dare to go inside of the haunted mansion, they could still stare in awe at the mark the Devil had left behind on the place. It was a stone face of a demon, its lips pulled back in a hideous snarl, looking out from the gable of the house. A reminder, some said, of the time when the Devil ate a meal in New Orleans!

Chapter Fourteen
No Escape... Even After Death

Ghostly Tales of Prisons & Jails in New Orleans

When compiling a list of the places in America where ghosts are most frequently found, prisons and jails are normally high on the list. The trauma, terror and pain experienced in a jail cell can leave a lasting impression, as can the terrible deeds that placed the men in these iron and stone cages. Even the horrible events that often occur in the prison can cause the spirits of the men who lived and died there to linger behind.

Nearly every jail is a scene of chaos. They are filled with noise at every hour of the day and night. The cells and corridors echo with shouting, laughter, crying, screaming, cursing and just about every other sound that a human can make. It is has often been said that these sounds can leave an indelible mark on the atmosphere of the location.

The city of New Orleans has been cursed with two locations where the prisoners of the past lingered for many years as the hauntings of the day!

Carrollton Jail

One of the most startling accounts of ghosts in New Orleans came from the old Carrollton Jail. During the years of 1898 and 1899, there were so many stories told of a haunting in the place that there remains little doubt that something very strange occurred in the building. To make matters even more credible, the majority of the witnesses who experienced these bizarre events were hard-boiled and credible officers of the law. Their realistic testimonies to the events in question make them all the more chilling.

This old structure, built around 1850, was officially known as the Jefferson Parish Prison, but more commonly, was simply called the "Carrollton Jail". Carrollton itself had come into existence around 1833 when a man named Charles Zimple laid out a town about five miles from the boundary of New Orleans. Zimple dubbed the new city "Carrollton" after

General William Carroll, a hero of the Battle of New Orleans. He had been encamped on the site of the future town with an army of Tennessee volunteers while awaiting orders from Andrew Jackson.

Two years after, the New Orleans and Carrollton Railroad was constructed to connect the city and the small town. The railroad is still used today as the St. Charles Avenue Streetcar line. It is the oldest, continually operating line of public transportation in America. The town was soon growing rapidly and by 1841, it was officially incorporated. Later, in 1852, it was named the county seat of Jefferson Parish and a handsome city hall and courthouse were built. They remain standing to this day, even though New Orleans eventually annexed the city in 1874.

Another part of the administrative collection of buildings was the parish prison. It stood on the corner of Hampson and Short Streets and after being built around 1852, it served as a jail until it was demolished in 1937. The brick building stood two stories tall and boasted large doorways and heavily barred windows. Most called it a "bleak and hideous place" and it was said that many of the prisoners met their ends here. Suicides were apparently quite frequent and disease and the lack of medical care added to the deaths. Violence, as with any prison, was also common. Still more of the prisoners had their fates decided on the gallows that were located in the square central courtyard. Many convicted thieves, rapists and murderers met justice at the end of the rope after being imprisoned in the narrow, stone cells of the jail. One lynching even took place in the courtyard after outraged citizens captured two men who had raped and butchered a little girl in the area.

These deaths and terrible events were said to have created a haunting at the Carrollton Jail.... a haunting that became a matter of public and official record. More than 50 years after the building was erected, the ghostly happenings at the jail became so persistent that they gained the attention of the newspapers of the day. On October 9, 1899, the first detailed reports about the supernatural in the parish prison appeared in print.

At that time, the prison was under the authority of Sergeant William Clifton, the Police Commander of the District. He had served with distinction for many years with the New Orleans Police Department and had taken over command of the jail in 1898. He was well respected and admired by those who served under him, including his clerk, a deputy, two doormen and eight patrolmen.

One summer evening, two men and a woman stopped by the jail to chat with Clifton. They came in through the great front entrance to the prison, which opened into a wide hallway. On the left side of the entryway was a door that opened into Clifton's office, a sparsely furnished room with a desk, a washstand, a sofa and a number of chairs. Behind Clifton's office, with a narrow passage between them, was the clerk's office. In this room were more desks and chairs and a wooden railing that divided the office.

As the woman that accompanied the men leaned against a wall in the office, she was immediately shoved out of the room as though someone had struck her violently. She spun into the hallway and was sent sprawling onto the floor. "Something pushed me!", she cried, her eyes wide with shock. "It pushed my shoulder away from the wall!"

Clifton and the men laughed and one of them joked about her getting old. A little angry about the fact that they didn't believe her, she leaned against the wall again. In seconds, she was sent reeling into the center of the room. Her body was flung into the cluster of men who were standing there and she was forced to take hold of them to keep from falling. This time, her face was pale with fear! "Something's in that wall!", she shouted at them. "I don't care what you say, somebody is there."

The men then took turns leaning against the wall and to their surprise, each was shoved away from it and toward the middle of the office. They carefully examined both sides of the wall but could find nothing to explain the strange event. What could have caused it?

Sergeant Clifton pondered the puzzle for a few moments and then his mind drifted back to an incident that he had heard about a few years before, prior to when he had come to work at the prison. A murderer, who had been arrested for boiling his wife in lye and making soap from her corpse, was arrested and brought to the jail. The story went that a number of angry police officers beat the man to death in the hallway outside of Clifton's office. His blood had been spattered all over the corridor. The story went that the killer swore he would be back to haunt the place. But had he?

Nonsense, Clifton told himself, there had to be a logical explanation for the wall. Or so he thought at that time. The events that followed would cause him to think differently!

A day or so later, Clifton was in his office with Corporal Perez, one of the patrolmen for the district. Their conversation turned to the portrait of General Beauregard that Clifton had hanging on his wall. He had always expressed an admiration for the general and in the course of his discussion, he turned to the portrait and gave it a quick salute. Immediately, with a great crash, the picture fell to the floor! At the same time, the washstand, with its bowl and pitcher, jumped forward and turned over. Strangely, nothing was broken. Even stranger, the heavy cord by which the portrait was hung was found to be in perfect condition. The nail in the wall was solid as well and even slanted upward. The two men, after close examination, could find no reason for the portrait to have fallen.

The following night, Clifton and Perez were telling some of the other officers about the strange happening. As he demonstrated what had occurred, he saluted the portrait once again. As soon as he did, the mirror that hung just below the general's picture flew from the wall. It also smashed into the wooden washstand, knocking everything to the floor. This time, the wash basin shattered into dozens of pieces but everything else remained intact. Clifton examined the mirror hanger and found that it was as strong as the one holding the portrait.

"It seemed as though invisible ears had been listening," Sergeant Clifton later reported, "and that unseen hands pushed the things from the wall.... I know that the portrait and the mirror could not have fallen unaided."

Several nights later, Clifton was sitting at his desk when he was suddenly held by the shoulders and his chair was spun completely around. At first he thought it was one of his men playing a joke, but when he turned to confront them, he found no one there! The room was fully lit and he could no one in the room or in the hallway. He questioned the doorman, but he replied that no one had come in the door.

And the spectral antics in the office didn't stop there!

The sofa in Clifton's office was frequently used by the patrolmen as a place to catch up on much-needed sleep during long shifts. One night, Officer Dell, who drove the patrol wagon, came in for a short nap. He had no sooner stretched himself out on the sofa before it lurched forward and out away from the wall. The bulky piece of furniture slid out about three feet and then suddenly reversed directions and thudded against the wall again. This was the same wall where the man had been beaten to death and the same one that was said to have flung the woman away and onto the floor.

Not long after that, another officer tried to rest on the couch. This time it not only slid out into the room, but it also tilted sharply and bounced the officer off in such a way that he collided with the corner of Clifton's desk and gashed his head open. Hearing his cry, Clifton rushed to his assistance and arrived just in time to see the couch sliding back against the wall again. The next night, another policeman, who boasted that he did not believe in ghosts, lay down on the couch in the presence of a number of other officers. Suddenly, the couch tipped up and the patrolman fell onto the floor! After that, the men began to stay far away from the couch until someone moved it to another part of the room. While the couch was again considered "safe", the patrolmen avoided that particular wall of the office for some time.

In October of that same year, a mounted officer named Jules Aucoin stepped into Sergeant Clifton's office to make a report. Clifton had stepped out for a few moments and Aucoin stood waiting for him near the desk. Just then, he saw a flash of movement out of the corner of his eye. He looked up quickly at a large, lithograph portrait of Admiral Dewey (a hero of the time period) that had been pasted on the wall.... the same wall that had been the center of much of the strange activity in the office. Before his eyes, Aucoin saw the portrait begin to spin like a wheel. It was as though someone had placed a nail through the center of the picture and then started rotating it! Keep in mind that such an act was virtually impossible as the portrait had been plastered onto the wall with strong glue.

Aucoin was stunned for a moment and then he ran out into the corridor and began shouting for his fellow officers. Those who were nearby came on the run, including Sergeant Clifton. As the men hurried into the office, they saw that the portrait had stopped moving and was in fact, affixed to the wall just as it had been. Aucoin explained what he had seen and the other men, having already witnessed other events for themselves, had no reason to doubt him.

Apparently though, the spirit of the wife-killer was not the only ghost who haunted the prison. Over time, all of the men who were stationed there reported strange and unexplainable noises, furniture and small objects moving about by themselves and falling without assistance, lights that turned on and off and much more. It's not surprising that these bizarre happenings tended to keep everyone on edge. Requests for transfers to other precincts were sent in frequently by officers who were stationed at the Carrollton Jail.

One night in autumn 1899, Corporal Harry Hyatt heard heavy footsteps in a nearby hallway. He stepped to the door of the Sergeant's office and looked around. Although he could still hear the sound of someone walking, he looked both ways down the corridor and found no one was about. The footfalls continued to sound and Hyatt noticed there was something odd about them. It seemed that each solid step was accompanied by another step that dragged, as though taken by a man who was lame. Hyatt also noticed that the corridor seemed to be filled with the faint smell of cigar smoke.

Finally, he left the doorway and walked out front. He asked the doorman, Officer Foster, if he had seen anyone come in. He shook his head until Hyatt described the sound that he heard in the hall. A faint memory stirred in Foster's mind and he grinned at Hyatt. "Maybe it was Harvey come back," he joked with his friend.

"Harvey" had been a gambler and a gigantic man, who walked with a severe limp. This didn't stop him from killing two racecourse jockeys by breaking their necks with his bare hands though. He also cut the tongues out of their horses. Apparently, he had wagered a small fortune on both of them and he was angry when they lost the races they were entered in. Harvey had been brought to the jail and had last been seen standing in the corridor in handcuffs with the cold stump of a cigar clenched between his teeth. Somehow, the man had vanished and had not been seen since. His escape from the jail left two dead guards, and a mystery, behind.

Hyatt shook his head. "Nope, he won't come back to see the inside of this jail," he laughed.

That evening, Hyatt picked up an evening newspaper and found a story about a gigantic man named Robert Brewer who had been found dead in a Pennsylvania town. He had been blind and lame but made a small living selling newspapers. After his death, they found a packet of papers among his effects that showed he was actually Harvey. The news story stated that he was wanted in New Orleans for four murders and elsewhere for other crimes.

Hyatt realized that Harvey had come back to the old prison after all!

The following night, at the same time, Hyatt again heard the shambling footsteps in the hallway. They plodded back and forth, back and forth. Hyatt went to the doorway, but there was still no one to be seen. "Okay, Harvey," he muttered to the empty space, "you can stop your pacing and smoke your cigar now".

The footsteps suddenly stopped. From out of thin air, a great cloud of tobacco smoke appeared about three feet from where Hyatt stood. It swirled and then slowly lifted off towards the ceiling and disappeared.

On another occasion, iron paperweights were raised from desks and flung at officers.

Icy cold chills appeared without explanation and always, there were the ghostly footsteps that sounded throughout the building. They paced the corridors and went up and down the stairs. One of the places especially affected by the sounds was the courtroom that was located on the second floor.

The room had been refurbished from the row of dark "condemned" cells that had once been located there. In these cages were kept the men who would soon die on the gallows. One night, very late, the footsteps became unusually strong and several officers followed them upstairs and into the courtroom. The room was eerie and silent, save for the tapping of the phantom boots. They circled the room as the police officers stood back and listened. Then, the footsteps stopped abruptly and the docket book, which was thick and weighed many pounds, flew from the judge's desk and crashed to the floor with such force that Sergeant Clifton heard it downstairs.

The footsteps were heard no more that night but Clifton had another encounter of his own that must have left him questioning the wisdom of remaining in command of the prison. In the early morning hours, he was seated at his desk when there suddenly came the grip of strong hands around his throat. He could feel the air being crushed out of him and he threw his arms up to ward off the attacker. His hands struck nothing but the attack immediately ceased. Clifton whirled around in his chair.... but there was no one behind him! No living person had entered his office, yet the marks of the hands could clearly be seen on his neck. In fact, mottled bruises remained there for some days after.

One afternoon, two quadroon girls appeared outside of the Sergeant's office and were spotted by Officer Foster. As the Sergeant was not in, he went over to speak to them. As he got close, they vanished before the man's eyes! It was believed that they were the ghosts of two young women who had been imprisoned there for carving out the liver of their mutual lover.

On another occasion, Foster also reported seeing a former prison officer named Sergeant Shoemaker standing alone in Clifton's office. The man stood near the desk for a moment and then bowed his head and walked slowly away. He got to within a foot of the sofa and then he too vanished! This was almost as surprising to Foster as the fact that he saw Shoemaker at all.... the man had been dead for over a year at this time!

Stories and reports would also bear out the fact that the officers were not the only ones to be bothered by the ghosts in the jail. In fact, one cell, Number Three, was infamous for the events that took place in it.

One night, a prisoner named Charles Marquez was brought in. All of the other cells were full, so he was placed in Number Three. The next morning, the guards found him lying on the floor of his cell, unable to stand and scarcely able to speak. His face was a mass of cuts and bruises and he looked as though he had been badly beaten. Clifton first assumed that one of the officers had beaten the poor man, but Marquez, once his wounds were treated, quickly convinced him otherwise. He claimed that he had been beaten by unseen hands... ghosts, he said, and that he had had been punched, kicked and pushed against the wall. Not once did he see his assailants and records did show that none of the prison personnel had been near the man's cell during the night.

Other prisoners soon got their own taste of Cell Number Three. Every criminal that was put into it told the same tale the next day and all of them had bruises and cuts to show that their claims were true. No one outside of the cell ever heard a thing, yet the occupant was always in sorry shape the next morning... and usually babbling about ghosts and monsters.

It was later learned that many years before, on a night when the prison was very crowded, three murderers were placed in Cell Number Three together. According to the story, they had fought all night, each man for himself, punching, biting and kicking the others. In the morning, two of them were dead and the third died before a priest could be called for him.

In 1937, the Carrollton Jail was finally torn down. Through its long life, the prison had been the scene of many ghostly tales and stories. Legend even had it that when the workmen demolished the structure, human shapes writhed in the clouds of dust, as though the creatures that had haunted the place now reveled in its destruction.

For years afterward, people in the area also claimed to hear the spectral sound of the gallows trap as it opened and sent another condemned man to his death. It is said that some older residents of the area claim the sounds of the gallows can still be heard today.

The Red-Headed Ghost of the Parish Prison

The old Parish Prison that was located at Tulane and Saratoga also had its own ghost stories. Back in the 1880's, a local newspaper reported that a number of prisoners had attempted suicide in one of the cells and that many of them had succeeded in ending their lives. The survivors cried of a red-haired woman who came down the corridor and entered the cell. She sadistically tortured them through the night until suicide became their only hope for release.

Each time that an emergency call came from that cell, whether the guards found the prisoner dead or merely frightened near to death, they would discover the cell door open and unlocked. They claimed that the red-headed ghost had been there and that she had opened the door.

Finally, after more than a dozen gruesome tragedies, the use of Cell Number Seventeen was discontinued. The cell was abandoned until the prison absorbed the Fourth Precinct Station. At that point, the cell was scrubbed and painted and put back into use. There were no more stories of ghosts or suicides connected to it.... but the ghost most certainly did not rest in peace!

Soon, stories began to be told of another cell, this one located up on the third floor of the City Prison portion of the building, at the corner of Orleans and Marais Streets. Over a period of just a few months, six different women attempted suicide in that particular cell. Each of them complained of a sinister red-headed woman who entered the cell and inflicted upon them such pain and agony that they tried to end their lives. Upon investigation, guards always found the cell door to be open, although the half-crazed occupant never seemed to notice or even care.

On other occasions, confused prisoners wandered into the offices of Captain Bachemin, the official in charge of the jail, and asked if they were free to go home. Each of them told the same bewildering story of a red-haired woman who unlocked their cell door and then told them to leave. The prisoners stated that she even went as far as to lead them down the corridor. When they turned to thank her, she had always vanished.

So, who was this strange and enigmatic creature?

One of the older guards recalled a story about a woman who had been incarcerated at the prison not long after it had opened. Her real name was unknown but she was always called "Countess Charlotte" and she had been housed in Cell Number Seventeen. She was said to have been very beautiful and charming enough to capture the attention of the Captain of the prison. He took to wandering past her cell each day and even took her out for a stroll in the evening as long as she was handcuffed to his wrist. One night, she tricked him and left him lying bleeding and unconscious in a Rampart Street room. She took his keys, his pistol and the handcuffs that she had been fastened with. Somehow, she managed to slip back into the prison and beat to death a turnkey on the stairs. She opened the cell doors and many of the prisoners, along with the "Countess" escaped.

She was captured again and brought back to the prison is less than a week. She was put back into her old cell, but she had no intention of staying there. In a crack in the wall, near the floor, she had hidden a long hatpin. Late at night, she took it out and wrapped a bit of cloth around one end of it. She then faced the stone wall and placed the point of the pin against her chest, carefully inserting it between her ribs. The "Countess" then rammed herself against the wall and thrust the pin straight into her heart. The guards found her the next morning, stiff and cold on the floor of the cell. She had never uttered a cry.

Was the Red-Headed Ghost only a legend? Perhaps she was, but what stands as fact is that more suicides took place in this prison than in any other jail in New Orleans. Was this twisted spirit really sending prisoners to their deaths... or could there be a more logical explanation?

The police officers at the old prison laughed at stories of ghosts, but as author Jeanne deLavigne wrote, they also "shuddered at the weird accounts and crossed themselves to ward off the evil influence of possible supernatural visitants."

†

Chapter Fifteen
Dinner, Lodging....
and Spirits

Haunted Hotels & Restaurants in New Orleans

New Orleans is a city that is known for being "something different". People come here in search of that elusive "something", from the local cuisine to the regional inns and hotels. The amount of history that is represented in New Orleans is often displayed in these establishments in the form of tradition, fine food and, not surprisingly, in ghost stories and hauntings. New Orleans boasts a number of locations where people eat, drink and even sleep alongside the denizens of the spirit world.

One of the best known of these locations is the **Lafitte Guest House**, one of the most charming of the guest houses in the French Quarter. It's located at the quiet end of Bourbon Street (yes, there is such a place!) and the ambience of the place definitely hearkens back to an earlier day. Some say that residents from these earlier times still linger behind. There are a couple of variations to the haunting, but one story claims that the resident ghost is that of the lady of the house, who originally owned the place in 1849. She is reportedly still watching over the house from the other side. Another tale promises a darker haunting and claims that a woman who lost her two daughters here many years ago haunts a particular room. Apparently, one of the girls perished from yellow fever and the other, unable to cope with the loss of her sister, ended her own life. Their ghostly mother is said to still cry for her children.

Another haunted inn is the **Andrew Jackson Hotel**, located on Royal Street. This quaint place, which can be found next door to the famous "Cornstalk Fence", is said to be haunted by the ghosts of children from the past. In 1794, this location was occupied by a boy's boarding school. It was destroyed by fire and according to the stories, five boys lost their lives in the blaze. Since that time, guests have reported hearing the sounds of boisterous children at play in the hotel. This is especially unusual as the hotel does not allow guests with children. Those who have complained about the noise, along with staff members, say the sounds come in the form of laughter, talking, yelling and even the occasional bloodcurdling scream.

Guests who stay at the **Olivier House** may have the chance to encounter a handful of different spirits. Several guests have been startled to run into a woman in antebellum clothing that often appears with a man in a Confederate uniform. However, they are not the most famous spirits in the house. That designation belongs to a spectral woman in black who wanders about the house and endlessly repeats the rosary. Many witnesses believe that she is simply another, albeit eccentric, guest until she vanishes before their eyes!

It is believed that this ghost is Madame Elizabeth Duparc Locoul, who purchased the property from Madame Olivier in 1836. Madame Locoul was known for being a devout Catholic, yet also had a reputation as a miser who mistreated her slaves. Her apparition has been seen most often in the first room of the hotel.

The buildings that now house **O'Flaherty's Irish Pub** were built in 1798 and held businesses with living quarters on the upper floors. The location has a long and sorted history that includes the use of one building as a quarantine house during a yellow fever epidemic, murder and suicide.

According to legend, Joseph Bapentier lived in a house here with his wife, Mary, in 1806. In 1810, he allegedly murdered a young woman on the property and then dumped her body into an old well. He committed suicide a short time later, although Mary resided here until her death in 1817. At that time, the property was auctioned off, but reportedly, the former owners never left. Mary Bapentier has been seen many times looking out a second floor window and the troubled spirit of her husband has been seen and felt a number of times in the courtyard.

Also encountered here is the ghost of the young woman who was murdered by Joseph Bapentier. She has been dubbed "Angelique", and has materialized in the courtyard as a girl of about 20 with long, brown hair. She has also been experienced as a mass of chilling air. According to reports, her spirit seems drawn to both young men and children and she enjoys stroking their hair and holding their hands.

Another spirited location is the **Provincial Hotel**, located on Chartres Street. During the Civil War, this building was used as a hospital for Confederate soldiers. The part of the present-day hotel that is referred to as "Building 5" was a ward for critically ill and maimed men. The trauma endured by these men has apparently left a lasting impression behind as it is the only part of the structure that is said to be haunted today. Staff members and guests have told of encounters with ghostly men on crutches, spectral doctors and surgeons and even bloodstains that mysteriously appear and then vanish.

A former brothel, the **Dauphine Orleans** also boasts more than its share of paranormal activity. A number of the original buildings here date back to 1775, including what is called the "Audubon Cottage", where artist John James Audubon painted his "Birds of America" in 1821. That structure is now used as the main meeting room for the hotel. While Audubon is not rumored to be hanging around the place, a number of other early residents are still said to be lingering in various portions of the hotel.

One such location is May Bailey's, the hotel bar, where the apparition of a man in a white suit and hat has been reported on a number of occasions. The ghost here is said to be responsible for knocking books off shelves in the lounge library, along with a number of other pranks. Another haunted spot is Suite 111, located above the bar, Here, objects are known for known for moving about on their own and guests have reported the spirit of a black man who has been nicknamed "George". It is said that when guests have forgotten to lock the door to the room, the ghost has taken care of it for them! Suite 110 also has it share of weirdness going on. Doors open and close here without explanation, lights turn on and off and the curtains to the room have a habit of opening by themselves.

The **Biscuit Palace**, which takes its names from the advertisement for Uneeda Biscuits that was painted in huge letters on the side, was once a private residence in the 1830's. Today, it offers modestly furnished apartments that can be rented on a temporary basis by visitors from out of town. Guests and staff members here have reported many strange occurrences over the years involving a pale, petite female apparition. She is completely benign and yet has a habit of rummaging through the clothing and dressers of occupants. Such incidents always take place when it would be impossible for anyone (living, that is) to have gotten into the rooms!

The **Commander's Palace** is a large, Victorian mansion that is located in the Garden District. Since 1880, it has been praised for its fine quality food and wonderful atmosphere. This being New Orleans, it's not surprising that it has a ghost or two around as well!

The restaurant was started in 1880 by Emile Commander and offered only the best food to the most distinguished families of the mostly American Garden District. It was opened at the corner of Washington Avenue and Coliseum Street on what was once the Livaudais Plantation. By 1900, it was attracting people from all over the country. Even through the 1920's, when it was under different management and served as a haven for gamblers and sporting gentlemen from the riverboats, it still maintained a family dining room downstairs. It was refurbished once in 1944 but when the Brennan family remodeled again in 1974 and gave the place a whole new look, stories of a resident ghost soon followed.

The restaurant is believed to be haunted by Emile Commander, the original owner of the place, and he is known to frequent one of the upstairs dining rooms that is known as the Sun Porch. One night, a table was set in advance for dinner guests and a bottle of wine was opened and poured into the glasses to allow the wine to breathe. When the host returned with the guests, about an hour later, one of the wine glasses was found to have been emptied. No one had been in or out of the room during the time the host was away.

Unexplained occurrences still continue to take place in the room, as well as in other parts of the building. Dishes and silverware are often moved and sometimes vanish to reappear again later, footsteps are heard pacing through the building at night, lights seem to have a mind of their own and glasses of liquor are often mysteriously drained. Staff members sometimes express a reluctance to discuss these odd events but all agree that the weird incidents are completely benevolent. There is little doubt in their minds that Emile Commander still considers the restaurant his own!

The Royal Cafe

The LaBranche House, which holds the Royal Cafe, is considered one of the most photographed buildings in the Vieux Carre, thanks to the exquisite ironwork that graces the structure. The property is located at the corner of Royal and St. Peter Streets and records date back to 1796. It was originally owned by Marianne Dubreuil, a free woman of color, although there were other structures here that were previously destroyed in the fires of 1788 and 1794. A wealthy sugar planter named Jean Baptiste LaBranche, who built the three-story structure here that can still be seen today, then purchased the land in 1832.

LaBranche was married to Marie Melanie Trepagnier and together, they had three sons. The house that still stands, after more than 170 years of hurricanes, floods and disasters, was built using the finest quality craftsmen. Marie LaBranche added the wrought iron balconies in 1842, after the death of her husband. It should be noted that she also managed to track down her husband's mistress that same year and, according to legend, murdered her!

The building was sold in 1866 to Paul Napoleon Rivera and he became the first of more than 30 different owners over the course of the next century. Previous owners always had strange tales to tell about the place.... as many claimed that it was haunted!

The Royal Cafe today is still said to be inhabited by ghosts. One of them is Marie LaBranche and the other is the unnamed mistress of Jean Baptiste LaBranche, who was murdered in 1842. According to some, the two of them have been doomed to remain together in this house for all eternity!

Mrs. LaBranche makes her presence known on the second floor of the restaurant, usually as a very strong and disconcerting presence. Many people who have dined here report feeling as though someone is standing directly over their shoulder, looking down on them. When they turn to look, they always discover that no one is there. She has also appeared as an apparition on rare occasions, wearing a dark blue dress and having long, styled hair. It is thought that her misdeeds in the house have tied her to the place.

The more active, and more restless, ghost in the house is that of the mistress. She is believed to be responsible for moving tables and chairs around but mostly makes her presence known on the third floor of the building. Here, she has rearranged furniture and has even thrown a coffee cup across a restaurant sales manager's desk.

According to the stories, she is believed to inhabit this area because she died here. It is said that after the death of LaBranche, his widow went to great efforts to learn the identity of the young woman that he had been having an affair with. Once discovered, Marie kidnapped her and brought her back to the house. She chained the woman to a wall in the attic and left her there to starve to death.

Today, this area is used as an office but strange things did not begin to happen here until it was renovated. Since that time, numerous electrical anomalies have been reported, including computer failures and lights turning on and off at strange times. There have also been cold spots encountered, along with doors opening and closing and the sound of footsteps that cannot be explained.

Antoine's Restaurant

There is perhaps no other restaurant in New Orleans that is as famous as Antoine's is. It was first established in 1840 and is now fifth-generation family owned. When New Orleans cuisine is talked about anywhere in the world, this is one of the first restaurants to come to mind. It has left an indelible mark on the city and because of this, it comes as no surprise to many that the world-famous restaurant also boasts a bevy of ghosts!

Antoine Alciatore came to New Orleans in 1840 after briefly working in the restaurant business in New York. He worked for a short time in the kitchen at the St. Charles Hotel and then started a boarding house and a restaurant. After he was established, he sent for his fiancee in New York and she came to New Orleans with her sister. After they were married, the two of them set to work making the restaurant the finest in the city. Their hard work paid off and soon, Antoine's outgrew its small quarters and moved down the block to its current location in 1868. In 1874, Antoine, in very poor health, left his family and returned to France. He passed away soon after, leaving a culinary legacy behind.

After the death of his father, Antoine's son, Jules, served as an apprentice under his mother before traveling to France, where he worked in the finest kitchens in Paris and Marseilles. In 1887, he returned to New Orleans and became the chef at the renowned Pickwick Club until his mother summoned him to master the kitchens at Antoine's. Jules later married Althea Roy, the daughter of a planter from Youngsville, and their son, Roy Louis, was born in 1902. They also had a daughter, considered the "grand dame" of the family, Marie Louise.

Roy Alciatore managed the restaurant for nearly 40 years, steering it through both the Prohibition Era and World War II. He passed away in 1972. Marie Louise married William Guste, and their sons, William Jr., former attorney general of Louisiana, and Roy Sr., became the fourth generation of the family to run the restaurant.

In 1975, Roy's son, Roy Jr., became the proprietor and operated Antoine's until 1984. He was followed by William's son, Bernard "Randy" Guste, who manages the place today. Through all of the changes though, the younger generations have had little to fear about making a mistake or not operating the restaurant according to the high standards of the family... because you see, at least one of the original Alciatore's has remained behind to keep an eye on things!

While several spirits are said to haunt Antoine's, the most visible and famous is that of the original owner himself. Guests and staff members have long confirmed the presence of Antoine's ghost, as sightings of the apparition bear an uncanny resemblance to the man who founded the restaurant more than 160 years ago. Even family members have encountered the ghost and believe that Antoine is still watching over his beloved eatery.

On one occasion, a family member was making some dinner preparations outside of the Japanese Room and happened to see what he thought was a busboy enter the room. As he followed the person, he reached for the door but found that it was locked. Curious now, he quickly unlocked the door and went inside to find it empty. However, there was no other way in or out of the room!

At another time, a relative was carrying some important documents to an upstairs office. As he was about to start climbing the stairs, he looked up to see a glowing figure on the landing above. The apparition had no real discernible features and gave off a dim light that prevented any details from being observed. Needless to say, the family member was quite surprised and could do little but stand there and gape at the image. Then, as mysteriously as it had come, the figure vanished!

A young staff person claimed to see Antoine enter the restaurant's Mystery Room. At first he thought the man, who he only got a glimpse of, was the headwaiter, so he followed him to ask a question that he needed an answer to. He followed into the dining room, but to his surprise, he found that no one was there. Returning to the front of the establishment, he saw the headwaiter and asked him where he had disappeared to so quickly. The headwaiter assured him that he had never left his post, despite the staff member's arguments that he had just seen him go into the Mystery Room.

When asked to describe the man that he had seen, the young waiter gave a remarkable description of Antoine Alciatore, even though he had no idea what the long deceased original owner had looked like. With a smile, the headwaiter informed him that he had just had a brush with the supernatural. The staff member vowed to never go into the Mystery Room again!

One night, a cashier spotted a man in a tuxedo standing in the dining room. This would not be completely out of the ordinary... except for the fact that the man was transparent! Within a moment or two, the figure vanished and no one fitting the man's description could be discovered in the restaurant.

The ghosts of Antoine's are a friendly sort and merely chose to remain behind in the place they knew and loved so well. Perhaps that is one of the finest recommendations that a restaurant can have... food so good that people return from the other side to eat there!

Chapter Sixteen
Brothers in Arms

Spirits of the Civil War at the Griffon House

Outside of the French Quarter, stands a house at 1447 Constance Street that has been haunted for as long as anyone in the neighborhood can remember. Whether it is still haunted or not, remains a question, but the stories that have been told about the place over the years can still manage to chill your blood.

The house on Constance Street was built in 1852 by Adam Griffon, who lived there for only a few years, abandoning the house when the Civil War came to New Orleans. It had been built as an elegant place with high ceilings and spacious rooms that were perfect for dress balls and fancy parties, but there was little in the way of festivity going on here in 1862 when the Federal Army took over New Orleans. When General Benjamin Butler's Union troops occupied the city in the early years of the war, they began selecting homes and buildings in which to house men and supplies. The house on Constance Street was one of the buildings selected for occupation.

However, the first soldiers who entered the house heard a chilling sound... that of rattling chains and groaning coming from upstairs. In the third floor attic, they found several slaves shackled to the wall and in a state of advanced starvation. Some of them even had untreated,

General Benjamin Butler

maggot-infested wounds. They were removed to a field hospital where they could be better taken care of and the house was turned into a barracks for soldiers and prisoners.

When Butler occupied New Orleans, he passed an order stating that anyone caught looting would be shot and this included his own Federal troops. Two Union officers were arrested for this offense and were confined to the house on Constance Street. They spent much of their time drinking whiskey that was given to them by sympathetic guards and singing over and over again the song "John Brown's Body".

This repetitive singing of a popular northern song was really a ruse to hide the fact that the men were actually Confederate deserters who had stolen the Union uniforms. They were wearing them when they were caught. They knew if they were discovered to be southerners, they would be killed, so they attempted to hide this fact by singing "John Brown's Body" over and over again.

When they learned that even Union soldiers caught looting would be shot, they bribed a guard to bring them a pair of pistols. They lay down beside each other on the bed, pointed the guns to one another's hearts and pulled the triggers at the same time. Their bodies were found the following morning, sprawled on a mattress so stained that the blood had actually seeped through the floorboards to the rooms below.

After the war, the building was used for commercial purposes as a lamp factory, a mattress factory and a perfume bottling plant. In the 1920's, it was a union hiring hall and one previous owner of the house was an old man who rebuilt air conditioners... until he disappeared one day without a trace. The old man always claimed that he had "seen things" in the house, but when pressured to elaborate, he always refused.

Over the years, there have been many reports of a haunting in the house. All through the various owners, the ghosts remained a constant force. Occupants spoke of hearing heavy boots coming from the third floor, the rattling of chains and screams from the dark attic. Neighbors and passersby also claimed to see two white-faced soldiers in blue uniforms standing at the third-floor window. Both of them were said to be holding a bottle in their hand and singing the words to "John Brown's Body".

Several incidents took place in 1936, during the period when the house was used a lamp factory. One night, a maintenance man was working there alone. It was just shortly before midnight and he was working on the second floor. To his surprise, a nearby door opened up on its own. As he stood there in shock, the sound of a pair of marching boots stomped into the room with him. Then, a second pair of boots joined the first and the pounding footsteps became almost deafening. Terrified, he scrambled for the staircase as the sound of the boots began to fade away. The footsteps were immediately followed by the spectral sound of drunken laughter and then the refrain of "John Brown's Body". The maintenance worker claimed to still be able to hear the horrifying voices as he ran down the street. Nothing, including the promise of increased wages, could convince him to return to the house again.

Shortly after taking possession of the house, the owner, Isadore Seelig, arrived at the factory one morning and was nearly killed. He and his brother were standing in the front hall talking when a huge concrete block was hurled at them from the head of the stairs.

"It didn't fall," Seelig later reported. "It was thrown. It never struck a stair as it came and it landed just where we had been standing. My brother saw it coming and pushed me out of the way. It probably would have killed us if it had hit us."

The two men charged upstairs to find out who was there and discovered the place to be empty. In one area, where the floors had been freshly painted the day before, they found not a single footprint.

""The upper windows and doors were all locked," added Seelig, "and when we went upstairs no one was there, and no one had been there. No such blocks had been used in any of the repairing around here either."

A few years later, when it seemed impossible to keep tenants in the place, the structure was turned into a boarding house for a brief time. A widow rented out one of the second floor rooms and settled in quite comfortably. Everything seemed very quiet for some time until one afternoon when she was sitting by the window with her sewing. She happened to look down and noticed that there was blood on her arm. Thinking that she must have accidentally scratched herself, she wiped the blood away but in an instant, it was back! Before she could wipe it off, another drop of blood appeared on her arm, then another, and another. She quickly looked up and saw the blood was oozing through a crack in the ceiling directly above where she was sitting. As she tried to understand what was happening, she heard an eerie sound coming from the third floor... the faint strains of "John Brown's Body" being sung by two drunken men!

The widow began to scream and she ran shrieking from the house, never to return. Her relatives later came back and packed up her household for her. They encountered no dripping blood in the house but as they were locking the front door, they claimed to see two soldiers in blue uniforms looking down at them from the attic window.

In the late 1970's, Kathleen and Anthony Jones bought the house with the intention of restoring it. In an interview with authors Richard Winer and Nancy Osborn, they said they had experienced nothing strange at the old place.... but for some reason, they never occupied the house.

Residents of the decaying neighborhood weren't speaking much after the 1970's, but one anonymous witness told an interesting story. He said that the rundown area (near a housing project) had deteriorated to the point that any abandoned house in the neighborhood had become fair game for drug addicts. The house at 1447 became one of these, but within a month, even the addicts had deserted it. They claimed they saw two white men there in "police uniforms" that walked through walls and sang "old timey songs"!

In more recent times, the house was sold to a local sculptor and his family and while they were aware of the haunted history of the house, they never witnessed anything supernatural.

Perhaps the two soldiers have finally found rest....
And then again, perhaps not.

Chapter Seventeen
The Sultan's Palace

The Haunted History of the Gardette - Le Prete Mansion

The Gardette-Le Prete Mansion, also known on occasion as the "Sultan's Palace", is one of the French Quarter's most imposing buildings and has always been a part of the city's legends and mysteries. According to the stories, it was once the scene of a brutal rape and violent bloodshed.... tragedies that still linger behind as a haunting.

A dentist named Dr. Joseph Coulon Gardette originally constructed the mansion on the corner of Orleans and Dauphine Street in the Vieux Carre. In 1825, it was the tallest house in the French Quarter, with basements that were further off the ground and ceilings that were higher than in any other private residence in the city. Four years after its completion, the house was sold to a wealthy Creole man named Jean Baptiste Le Prete. He made the house even more extravagant by adding the cast-iron grillwork to the balconies, which has become the mansion's most distinguishing feature. With its top floor ballroom and spacious galleries, the house came to be regarded as one of the most luxurious mansions in New Orleans. Not surprisingly, it became the center of Creole culture in the French Quarter of the middle 1800's.

Unfortunately, the wealth and power of many of the Creole families started to decline in the second half of the century, leading many to scandal and ruin. Le Prete was one of those who lost much of his fortune and he found that he was forced to rent out his wonderful home in 1878.

His tenant was a mysterious Turk who claimed to be a deposed Sultan of some distant land. A short time before, a vessel of war had arrived in the New Orleans harbor at night. Men came and went from the ship on official business and finally, a wealthy Oriental man, dressed in a regal costume, came ashore and was received with great respect by city officials. Le Prete was called into a private conference and was asked if his property might be available for lease. He agreed to the generous terms offered, not realizing the dangerous conditions he was bringing to the mansion.

According to what he could learn, the "Sultan" was a deposed ruler from a distant Asian country. It seemed that he had fled the land with his brother's favorite wife. He had hidden away in Europe for a time and then had sailed for New Orleans. He had brought with him his entire entourage, including armed guards and a harem of women. These women were of all ages and sizes and rumors said that the harem also included young Arab boys, who fulfilled the Sultan's more unseemly desires.

Le Prete had to take his wife and children, along with all of their belongings, and vacate the house completely. They went to live on their plantation while the Sultan went about transforming the house into an eastern pleasure palace. The Turk had transported with him a fortune in gold and established a line of credit at all of the banks. He used his wealth to begin work on the mansion. Soon, the floors were covered with carpets from Persia, soft couches were embroidered with colorful patterns, cushions were piled high in the corners and carefully carved furniture, chairs and chests were picked up from the docks. Soon, the move was complete and candles were lighted and braziers were heated to warms the rooms. The smell of heavy incense filled the air and passersby could hear the laughter of the women and their soft voices as they walked in the courtyard each day. Their foreign tongues tantalized the neighborhood men, as did the rustle of their rare silk garments.

And yet no one ever saw these beautiful women. Complete privacy was maintained at all times. The doors and windows were covered and blocked, the gated front portal was never opened and men patrolled the grounds with curved daggers in their belts. The iron gates around the property were chained and locked and the house became a virtual fortress.

Neighbors began to talk, their curiosity aroused by the strange and forbidding changes to the house. A few weeks before, the place had been open and filled with light but now was dark and menacing. They didn't have time ponder these changes for long though because a short time later, all of it was destroyed!

A few months passed and one night, a terrible storm crashed over the city. Under the cover of darkness, an unfamiliar ship with a strange, crescent banner sailed into the harbor. In the morning, it was gone and it had taken the storm with it.

That morning, neighbors passing by the mansion noticed that trickles of blood were running out from under the iron gates. The authorities were summoned but could raise no one, so they forced open the doors and went inside. Here, they found the gate to the courtyard standing wide open on its hinges and muddy footprints leading in and out of the house. The people from the neighborhood soon found the first indication of the horror that awaited them in the bodies of a few servants had been slashed with swords and left for dead. They cautiously entered the house and found absolute carnage.

At some point in the night, a massacre had taken place. Blood splattered the floors and walls, headless bodies and amputated limbs were scattered about and all of them had been butchered by sword or ax. No room was without a horrific scene. The bodies and limbs were scattered about, mutilated and burned in such a way that no one could learn which bodies belonged to what person. No exact count of the dead was ever determined.

The Gardette-Le Prete House during its decline.

And the horror didn't stop with murder... the beautiful harem girls, the Arab boys, the Sultan's children and even the guards, were raped and subjected to vile sexual assaults. The scandal was so horrendous that the details of that night have still not been chronicled completely to this day!

The Sultan's mutilated body was found in the garden, where he had been buried alive. In his struggle to free himself from his earthen prison, he managed to partially tear himself from the grave, but it was not enough. He still choked to death on mouthfuls of pungent earth. Over his hasty grave, a marble tablet was placed, bearing an inscription in Arabic. It read: "The justice of heaven is satisfied, and the date tree shall grow on the traitor's tomb". It is said that a tall tree did indeed grow on this spot and was known locally as "the tree of death".

While the tree has long ago perished, the legends of the house remain. The identity of the murderers was never discovered. Some say they were the members of some pirate's crew who had business with the mysterious Sultan and some say the crimes were the work of the Turk's own brother, seeking revenge for the theft of his wife and of the family wealth.

But I don't imagine we will ever really know.....

What we do know is that the Le Prete mansion came to be regarded as a haunted house... and one infested by ghosts! For many years, the mansion was almost a slum dwelling as the owners did little to maintain the place. It was even rented out as apartments during the great influx of Italian immigrants in the late 1800's. During this period of its worst decay, an Italian woman who lived there washed her clothes and then hung them out to dry on the top gallery. One day she fell over the ironwork and to the pavement below, and was instantly killed. She most likely leaned back too far while hanging the clothes on the line but other tenants in the building blamed the spirits for her death. She was pushed, they would say.

In 1949, the building housed the New Orleans Academy of Art for a brief time but the whispers of ghosts and hauntings never really stopped. The stories said that strange sounds could often be heard there at night, like the soft piping of Oriental flutes and the pad of footsteps on the stairs. It was also believed that the faces of the women in the Sultan's harem could sometimes be seen peering out of windows on the upper floors. Screams, moans and frantic running sounds were also commonly reported.

By the 1950's, the house was once again used as an apartment building and refurbished. It was now divided into nine units, several of which were two-storied. Still, the tales of ghosts lived on!

One of the reports came from tenants in the house during the 1950's. In a newspaper interview, one tenant stated that she had been startled numerous times by a man in a garish Oriental costume. The man would then disappear as mysteriously as he came. She, and others, also reported hearing footsteps in the hallways and screams echoing inside of the rooms.... as if the terrible events of yesterday were still taking place there!

On one occasion, the previously mentioned tenant heard the sounds of a man's violent and blood-curdling screams emanating from the bottom of a dark spiral staircase. She was with a friend on that occasion and not only did they not go down to see if anyone was there, but they both left the building immediately and never returned. The tenant moved out a short time after.

Roughly ten years later, a woman named Jean Damico and her husband, Frank, purchased the house in 1966. They had decided to restore the place and turn it into luxury apartments. Soon after, neighbors began to tell Jean about the house's bizarre history and the bloody incidents that had taken place there. She dismissed the stories as nothing more than supernatural gossip... until she had her own experiences there!

One night, while trying to sleep, Jean sensed a presence in the room with her. She looked up and saw a man standing at the end of the bed. As she reached for the bedside lamp, and filled the room with light, the apparition vanished.

And that was the last thing heard from Jean Damico. According to recent reports, she still resides in the old mansion, although she has no further interest in talking about ghosts!

Regardless, the "Sultan's Palace" remains a curious and intriguing mystery of New Orleans and the French Quarter. We may never know what secrets this old mansion still hides... although the spirits that inhabit this place just might know them. Perhaps if someone would listen, what strange tales they would have to tell!

Troy Taylor works hard to unearth new hauntings and to keep the old lore alive. In spite of this, many of the stories which shaded our cemeteries and lingered over our abandoned buildings are forever lost. So while some of us will wonder about the light burning in the old warehouse, or quicken our step in a dusky graveyard, or pause to make sure those are our own footsteps echoing off the attic wall, most of us won't.

Yesterday's stories, like yesterday's spirits, draw their power from being remembered. In the absence of memory, legends die, and like forgotten ghosts are left to fade away.

Joe Richardson
Illinois Country Living Magazine

Select Bibliography & Recommended Reading

Ainbinder, Sheila - LEGENDS OF LOUISIANA COOKBOOK (1987)
Arthur, Stanley Clisby - OLD NEW ORLEANS (1936)
Asbury, Herbert - THE FRENCH QUARTER (1936)
Bruce, Curt - THE GREAT HOUSES OF NEW ORLEANS (1977)
Bultman, Bethany Ewald - NEW ORLEANS (1998)
Carter, Hodding - PAST AS PRELUDE: NEW ORLEANS 1718-1968 (1968)
Clark, Sandra Russell - ELYSIUM: A GATHERING OF SOULS (1997)
Cohen, Daniel - IN SEARCH OF GHOSTS (1972)
deLavigne, Jeanne - GHOST STORIES OF OLD NEW ORLEANS (1946)
Dickinson, Joy - HAUNTED CITY (1995)
Ellms, Charles - THE PIRATES (1996)
Fate Magazine (various editions)
Florence, Robert - CITY OF THE DEAD (1996)
Florence, Robert - NEW ORLEANS CEMETERIES (1998)
Fox, F.G. - BIZARRE NEW ORLEANS (1997)
Garvey, Joan B. & Mary Lou Widmer - BEAUTIFUL CRESCENT (1984)
Ghosts of the Prairie Magazine (Various editions)
Ghosts of the Prairie Website: "Haunted New Orleans" (www.prairieghosts.com)
Guiley, Rosemary Ellen - ENCYCLOPEDIA OF GHOSTS & SPIRITS (1993)
GUMBO YA-YA - Lyle Saxon, Edward Dreyer, Robert Tallant / WPA Project (1945)
Harper's Weekly Magazine - THE SOUTH (collected in 1990)
Hauck, Dennis William - HAUNTED PLACES: THE NATIONAL DIRECTORY (1996)
Holzer, Hans - GOTHIC GHOSTS (1970)
Huber, Leonard V. - NEW ORLEANS: A PICTORIAL HISTORY (1975)
Jones, Big Ray - COMPLETE IDIOT'S GUIDE TO NEW ORLEANS (1998)
Kane, Harnett - QUEEN NEW ORLEANS: CITY BY THE RIVER (1949)
Klein, Victor C. - NEW ORLEANS GHOSTS (1993)
Klein, Victor C. - NEW ORLEANS GHOSTS II (1999)
Konstam, Angus - HISTORY OF PIRATES (1999)
Leblanc, Guy - IRREVERENT GUIDE TO NEW ORLEANS (1998)
Lynn, Stuart - NEW ORLEANS (1949)
Martinez, Raymond - MYSTERIOUS MARIE LAVEAU VOODOO QUEEN (1956)
Mugnier, George Francois - NEW ORLEANS AND BAYOU COUNTRY (1972)

Myers, Arthur - THE GHOSTLY REGISTER (1986)
New Orleans Times-Picayune Newspaper (Various editions)
NOLA / New Orleans website (www.nola.com) Special thanks to articles by Jim Krane
Norman, Michael & Beth Scott - HAUNTED AMERICA (1994)
Pelton, Robert W. - VOODOO CHARMS AND TALISMANS (1973)
Pyle, Howard - BOOK OF PIRATES (1903)
Reader's Digest - INTO THE UNKNOWN (1981)
Reader's Digest - MYSTERIES OF THE UNEXPLAINED (1982)
Roberts, Nancy - AMERICA'S MOST HAUNTED PLACES (1976)
Rogo, D. Scott - AN EXPERIENCE OF PHANTOMS (1974)
Rose, Al - STORYVILLE   NEW ORLEANS (1974)
Saxon, Lyle - FABULOUS NEW ORLEANS (1928)
Scherts, Helen Pitkin - LEGENDS OF LOUISIANA (1922)
Sifakis, Carl - ENCYCLOPEDIA OF AMERICAN CRIME (1982)
Smith, Susy - PROMINENT AMERICAN GHOSTS (1967)
Spaeth, Frank - PHANTOM ARMY OF THE CIVIL WAR (1997)
Stanforth, Diedre & Louis Reems - ROMANTIC NEW ORLEANS (1977)
Tallant, Robert - VOODOO IN NEW ORLEANS (1946)
Tallant, Robert - MURDER IN NEW ORLEANS (1953)
Taylor, John Gray - LOUISIANA: A BICENTENNIAL HISTORY (1976)
Taylor, Troy - GHOST HUNTER'S GUIDEBOOK (1999)
Winer, Richard & Nancy Osborn - HAUNTED HOUSES (1979)
Winer, Richard - GHOST SHIPS (2000)
Wlodarski, Rob and Anne - SOUTHERN FRIED SPIRITS (2000)

Personal Interviews & Correspondence
Special Thanks to my favorite Ghost & Cemetery Tour Co. in New Orleans:
Magic Walking Tours 588-9693

About The Author: Troy Taylor

Troy Taylor is the author of 15 previous books about ghosts and hauntings in America, including HAUNTED ILLINOIS, SPIRITS OF THE CIVIL WAR, THE GHOST HUNTER'S GUIDEBOOK. He is also the editor of GHOSTS OF THE PRAIRIE Magazine, a travel guide to haunted places in America. A number of his articles have been published here and in other ghost-related publications.

Taylor is the president of the "American Ghost Society", a network of ghost hunters, which boasts more than 450 active members in the United States and Canada. The group collects stories of ghost sightings and haunted houses and uses investigative techniques to track down evidence of the supernatural. In addition, he also hosts a National Conference each year in conjunction with the group which usually attracts several hundred ghost enthusiasts from around the country.

Along with writing about ghosts, Taylor is also a public speaker on the subject and has spoken to well over 100 private and public groups on a variety of paranormal subjects. He has appeared in literally dozens of newspaper and magazine articles about ghosts and hauntings. He has also been fortunate enough to be interviewed over 300 times for radio and television broadcasts about the supernatural. He has also appeared in a number of documentary films like AMERICA'S MOST HAUNTED, BEYOND HUMAN SENSES, GHOST WATERS, NIGHT VISITORS and in one feature film, THE ST. FRANCISVILLE EXPERIMENT. He also currently has a television series in the works with GASLIGHT PICTURES in Hollywood.

Born and raised in Illinois, Taylor has long had an affinity for "things that go bump in the night" and published his first book HAUNTED DECATUR in 1995. For six years, he was also the host of the popular, and award-winning, "Haunted Decatur" ghost tours of the city for which he sometimes still appears as a guest host. He also hosts the "History & Hauntings Tours" of Alton, Illinois.

In 1996, Taylor married Amy Van Lear, the Managing Director of Whitechapel Press, and they currently reside in a restored 1850's bakery in Alton.

Whitechapel Productions Press

History & Hauntings Book Co.

Whitechapel Productions Press was founded in Decatur, Illinois in 1993 and is a publisher and purveyor of books on ghosts and hauntings. We also produce the "Ghosts of the Prairie" Magazine and the "Ghosts of the Prairie" Internet web page. We are also the distributors of the "Haunted America Catalog", the largest specialty catalog of ghost books in the United States.

Call us Toll-Free for More Information at
1-888-Ghostly

Or visit us On-line at the Ghosts of the Prairie Web Page at www.prairieghosts.com

Current Publications from Whitechapel Productions Press

HAUNTED ILLINOIS: GHOSTS AND HAUNTINGS FROM EGYPT TO THE WINDY CITY BY TROY TAYLOR (1999) Haunted Illinois is a chilling trip through the haunted history of Illinois! Discover the dark side of the Prairie State with more than 80 tales of ghosts and the unexplained, many of which have never appeared in print before! Join the author on a trip like no other you have ever taken before with tales that span the entire history of the state and various regions of Illinois. Locations and tales include: The Old Slave House; Allerton Mansion; Pemberton Hall; Voorhies Castle; Ghosts of Springfield; Haunted Alton; the Watseka Wonder; Bartonville State Hospital; Haunted Chicago; Resurrection Mary; Bachelor's Grove Cemetery and literally dozens more! $19.95

HAUNTED DECATUR REVISITED BY TROY TAYLOR (2000) Journey back in time with author Troy Taylor as he takes you into the dark side of Central Illinois and reveals the "Land of Lincoln" in way that no other book has done before. Explore the ghosts and haunted places of Springfield, Champaign, Bloomington, the dozens of small towns of the prairie, and of course, Decatur... the epicenter for hauntings and strange activity in the region! Discover the ghosts and haunted places of Decatur and Central Illinois and explore new places, new stories and new haunted spots from the original HAUNTED DECATUR, GHOSTS OF SPRINGFIELD and beyond! Includes stories never in print before! We dare you to read this book... you'll never look at the Haunted Heart of Illinois in the same way again! $18.95

THE GHOST HUNTER'S GUIDEBOOK BY TROY TAYLOR (1999) THE ESSENTIAL HANDBOOK FOR INVESTIGATING GHOSTS & HAUNTINGS! This must-have guide solves not only the mysteries of finding haunted places, but what to do when you discover them! Larger and more complete that any other ghost hunting manual you have seen before, it is the ultimate guide for paranormal investigations, written by a real-life ghost hunter with years of experience in tracking down the paranormal. In addition to providing a step-by-step guide to conducting your own paranormal investigations, this book also features sections on ghost detection equipment, spirit photography, EVP, interviewing witnesses and much more! $12.95

SEASON OF THE WITCH by TROY TAYLOR (1999) The Haunted History of the Bell Witch of Tennessee! Explore one of the most famous hauntings in American History... the Infamous Bell Witch of Tennessee! One of the most comprehensive volumes ever written about this fascinating case... and one you won't want to miss! Journey along with author Troy Taylor as he leads you back through the original facts of the case, using eye-witness accounts and first-hand observations of the Bell Witch and her strange activities. Delve into the possible solutions to the case and the theories about who the witch really was! Then discover how the strange events of the case continued to echo in Robertson County, Tennessee for many years after the haunting began.... and find out why many believe they still continue today! Explore the shadowy depths of the Bell Witch Cave, from the 1800's to the tales which are told today! $13.95

SPIRITS OF THE CIVIL WAR BY TROY TAYLOR (1999) A GUIDE TO THE GHOSTS & HAUNTINGS OF AMERICA'S BLOODIEST CONFLICT.... Join author Troy Taylor on a spell-binding journey through the horrific events of the Civil War! Meet the lingering spirits of the past and discover the places where the dead still walk today! This is a fascinating guide to both the strange history and the ghostly locations of the war and includes many tales which have never been told before.... plus haunts from classic locations where the soldiers of yesterday have not found rest! Travel along as the author introduces you to dozens of haunted locations in both the north and south... including historic homes; private residences; forts; field hospitals and prisons! Witness the haunts of slavery and the Underground Railroad! Uncover the secrets and the spirits of the Lincoln Assassination; and of course, the blood-curdling accounts of the war's most haunted battlefields, including Antietam, Chickamauga and a special section on the Spirits of Gettysburg! $17.95

HAUNTED ALTON: HISTORY & HAUNTINGS OF THE RIVERBEND REGION (2000) Take a journey through the dark side of Alton, Illinois with author and ghost researcher, Troy Taylor! Discover the hidden past of the Riverbend Region and its haunted history of death, the Civil War, the Underground Railroad, murder, disease and strange deeds... and learn how the events of yesterday have created the hauntings which still linger in the city today. This is the first book solely written about the ghosts of Alton! Read More About Haunted Alton! $14.95

WINDY CITY GHOSTS BY DALE KACZMAREK (2000) TRUE TALES FROM AMERICA'S MOST HAUNTED CITY! Windy City Ghosts is a spell-binding journey to the haunted places of Chicago, America's Most Haunted city! Join author and real-life ghost researcher Dale Kaczmarek as he takes you on a personal trip to the Windy City's most haunted sites, including homes, churches, cemeteries and even Chicago landmarks! This is a must-have guide to ghosts and hauntings and includes tales which have never appeared in print before! Includes dozens of photographs and results from genuine paranormal investigations! The ultimate look at Chicago ghosts! $16.95

 Upcoming from Author Troy Taylor

BEYOND THE GRAVE: AMERICA'S HAUNTED GRAVEYARDS
The Haunted History of the spookiest graveyards in America is explored in this long-awaited book by Troy Taylor. Journey to the darkest corners of our landscape in search of ghosts, eerie legends and more!

GHOSTS ALONG THE RIVER ROAD
Take a winding trip along the Mississippi River in search of ghosts, hauntings and some of America's greatest legends with author Troy Taylor

HAUNTED HISTORY: GHOSTS OF THE PRAIRIE
Troy Taylor's "Haunted History" series finally begins with an exploration of the ghosts and hauntings of the American Midwest!

Printed in the United States
63202LVS00004B/17